The first years at school

Developing Teachers and Teaching

Series Editor: **Christopher Day**, Reader in Education Management and Director of Advanced Post-Graduate Courses in the School of Education, University of Nottingham.

Teachers and schools will wish not only to survive but also to flourish in a period which holds increased opportunities for self-management – albeit within centrally designed guidelines – combined with increased public and professional accountability. Each of the authors in this series provides perspectives which will both challenge and support practitioners at all levels who wish to extend their critical skills, qualities and knowledge of schools, pupils and teachers.

Current titles:

Angela Anning: *The First Years at School*
Les Bell and Chris Day (eds): *Managing the Professional Development of Teachers*
Joan Dean: *Professional Development in School*
C. T. Patrick Diamond: *Teacher Education as Transformation*
John Elliott: *Action Research for Educational Change*

The first years at school

Education 4 to 8

Angela Anning

Open University Press
Milton Keynes · Philadelphia

Open University Press
Celtic Court
22 Ballmoor
Buckingham
MK18 1XW

and
1900 Frost Road, Suite 101
Bristol, PA 19007, USA

First Published 1991

British Library Cataloguing in Publication Data

Anning, Angela
    The first years at school: education 4 to 8. –
    (Developing teachers and teaching series).
    1. England. Primary education
    I. Title II. Series
    372.942

    ISBN 0-335-09592-5 (pb)
    ISBN 0-335-09593-3 (hb)

Library of Congress Cataloging-in-Publication Data

Anning, Angela, 1944–
    The first years at school: education 4 to 8/Angela Anning.
        p.   cm.
    Includes bibliographical references and index.
    ISBN 0-335-09592-5 (pb) ISBN 0-335-09593-3 (hb)
    1. Education, Preschool—Great Britain. 2. Education, Elementary—
    Great Britain.   I. Title.
    LB1140.25.G7A55   1991
    372.21′0941—dc20   90–14189
                                                              CIP

Typeset by Rowland Phototypesetting Limited
Bury St Edmunds, Suffolk
Printed in Great Britain by St Edmundsbury Press Limited
Bury St Edmunds, Suffolk

For Vicky and Simon who taught me most of all

Contents

Series editor's introduction

This book is the first of its kind on the education of 4–8-year-old children. It will, I am certain, become 'required reading' for all teachers in training, and all those serving teachers who want to take stock of their current thinking and practices. The book has grown out of Angela Anning's twenty years' experience of working alongside and talking with primary teachers and demonstrates a broad and detailed knowledge of research and other commentaries on the state of schooling for this most important cohort of children. In a very real sense, then, it is both practical and reflective.

In reviewing the historical and ideological traditions of British infant and primary schools and nursery education, she characterizes infant teachers of the 1990s as being caught between child-centred progressivism and the utilitarian demands of the Elementary School tradition. In her discussion of views of children's learning, the author presents a valuable detailed and authoritative critique of accepted thinking about the cognitive, social and emotional development of children. Citing recent classroom-based research she emphasizes the need for teachers to intervene more to extend children's thinking in contexts which are familiar to them; she also makes a vital distinction between the need for teachers to take account of each child's past learning experiences which are different and their need to recognize that not every child learns differently. Allied with this, Anning details, through careful argument and examples of teachers in action in the classroom, the complexities of the teacher's roles, particularly the use of language intervention, role-modelling and expectations. She discusses the curriculum in practice, the effects of different models of organization and structures. She argues the need for teachers to offer moral frameworks to children beneath the visible surface of practice.

The final chapters of the book deal explicitly with the National Curriculum and its assessment. The author is critical of 'vague descriptions' of achievement specified in attainment targets, but is much more optimistic about the programmes of study for the core subjects. These she sees as being 'reassuringly in line with good practice'. She acknowledges the opportunities which the 'new curriculum' offers to teachers to be analytical in addressing the need to re-examine current culture, traditions and craft knowledge in early years education. Finally, she argues forcibly for equal opportunities for children with special needs, for equal treatment of boys and girls, for equal access to quality educational opportunities for the pre-fives, and in particular for increased status for teachers.

The book is filled with practice-based knowledge about the curriculum, children, and teaching and learning. As such it should commend itself to all who have an interest in promoting quality education through the management, planning, teaching and assessment of the curriculum for 4–8-year-olds in the 1990s and beyond.

Christopher Day

Preface

The 1990s promise to be a period of tumultuous changes in schools in the UK. Under the terms of the Education Reform Act 1988 a National Curriculum is to be laid down for all children aged 5 to 16 in state schools. Children are to be tested at ages 7, 11, 14 and 16. Local financial management will introduce a new element of control to governing bodies in the financing and running of schools. All these radical changes will be introduced as the 1990s unfold.

Yet the infant schools within which I work with teachers and students will carry forward, with any changes imposed by outsiders, a history and culture which underpin the new initiatives. This book was written with the intention of clarifying why things are as they are in infant schools. It also aims to explore some of the exciting new areas of research into the processes of educating young children. But my principal concern is that it is important that we understand why we are as we are in order that we may speculate about and gain some control over what might happen next.

I would like to make it clear that my analysis of classroom practices is as much an attempt to understand my own dilemmas as a teacher of young children as it is to offer more distanced observations of infant teachers and pupils at work. I have a deep sense of commitment to the education of young children, and a loyalty to the teachers with whom I have worked. I have never forgotten how much of the personal is expressed in the day-to-day functioning of a professional educator at work and how debilitating self-doubts can be; so my hope is that the questions I raise will not be seen as destructive criticism.

This quotation from Penelope Lively best crystallizes my feelings about the teachers and pupils I have known:

> You are public property – the received past. But you are also private; my view of you is my own, your relevance to me is personal.
> (Penelope Lively, *Moon Tiger*, Penguin, 1988: 29)

Histories and ideologies

An analysis of the past can help us to understand what is happening now and to anticipate what may happen in the future in schools. Just as every teacher's behaviour in school is influenced by his or her own personal and professional experiences, so every school is influenced by a range of local, political, economic and personnel changes and in turn every LEA is influenced by wider political and social changes. An awareness of these imperatives can make things that are happening in schools that appear incomprehensible suddenly become clear. Anybody who has moved to a new job recently and has struggled through the period of adjustment to an alien working culture will testify to this process of dawning enlightenment as past histories, conveyed through staffroom talk, clarify all manner of idiosyncratic school rules and habits. These flashes of insight are reassuring. Understanding how and why situations have arisen can help the individual to come to terms with uncomfortable current realities. In this chapter changes within the historical and ideological traditions of British primary and infant schooling will be reviewed. A discussion of the past will serve to illuminate some of the habits and assumptions underlying infant school practice today and give some insights into what may happen in the future.

Historical perspectives

In Britain infants from the age of 3 were admitted to schools throughout the nineteenth century. For many this meant attending the notorious dame schools, often bleak childminding provision for working mothers. Others were sent with older brothers and sisters to the monitorial schools. The 'babies

class' for pre-5-year-olds and the infant class for children over 5 might take sixty
to eighty children. The children sat in the fixed, tiered galleries that contem-
porary children in their projects about 'schooling long ago' love to role-play . . .
for an hour or so! Sitting still for day after day with older children drilling them
in writing (always with the right hand), letter recognition, object recognition
lessons and copying objects for drawing lessons must have been a tedious way
for such young children to spend their days. In more enlightened times,
practical activities recommended by Froebel (1826), one of the great inno-
vators in nineteenth-century education to whom we shall return later in the
chapter, were introduced into the curriculum, but these activities were done in
unison, with perhaps one child in each row handling by rote the soft spheres,
wooden spheres, cylinders and cubes and boxes of shapes which make up the
Froebel 'gifts' as the teacher called out instructions. The physical constraints of
sitting still were relieved only by drill or marching lessons in the school yards.

A handful of more fortunate children attended the few free kindergartens
which were set up by various charitable trusts for slum children in Salford,
London and Edinburgh. In these philanthropic institutions the emphasis was
on physical and medical care. In 1816 Robert Owen, as manager of a cotton mill
in Scotland, pioneered the New Lanark Infant School. Owen had visited Jean
Pestalozzi's school in Switzerland. Pestalozzi emphasized the importance of
children learning through experience and deplored rote learning (see Curtis
and Boultwood 1962). Owen was impressed with the Pestalozzi school and
based the curriculum of the New Lanark Infant School on similar principles.
The children were divided into two age groups (2–4-year-olds and 4–6-year-
olds) before they went into the schoolroom at 7 – the equivalent of Standard
1 in the elementary schools. The emphasis was on outdoor play, nature
study, music, dancing and (perhaps in deference to our colonial aspirations)
geography.

Infant schools were set up in many of the major cities from 1818 onwards.
They were seen as agents of moral and social rescue and training and
emphasized rote learning of reading, writing and numeracy, sewing and
manual dexterity activities in the classrooms and physical training in the
playgrounds. Many of them were under the auspices of various denominations
of the church; in general a tone of moral righteousness pervaded both the
textbooks and the teacher attitudes. The National Society for the Education of
the Poorer Classes in the Principles of the Established Church set up in 1811
was the kind of body that influenced the beginnings of the British elementary
school tradition.

From the middle of the nineteenth century state funds were allocated to
assist in the establishment of a national system of education. From 1833 small
state grants were offered towards the buildings of some schools. As public
funds were released, demands for accountability grew. In 1858 a Commission
was appointed under the chairmanship of the Duke of Newcastle 'to enquire
into the present state of popular education in England and to consider and

report what measures, if any, are required for the extension of sound and cheap elementary instruction to all classes of the people'. The results of the Royal Commission were published in 1861. By the terms of the Revised Code their recommendations were put into effect in 1862. Children were first formally tested within schools in Standard 1 at 7. Teachers were paid according to the results their pupils gained in the standard tests, as well as on minimal attendance – hence the still evident neuroticism in schools about registers. Schools were inspected by HMIs to ensure that they were conforming to the requirements of the code.

In the summer of 1870 both Houses of Parliament debated the compulsory school starting age. One argument claimed that 'five was a tender age for compulsory attendance'; another that 'it was never too early to inculcate habits of decency, cleanliness and order' (quoted in Whitbread 1972). In the end the clinching argument was that 'The difficulty was to obtain education without trenching on the time for gaining a living: beginning early and ending early would present a solution' (NEU 1870: 441–2). On this instrumental note the English education system's unique policy of entry to school at the age of 5 was established.

The curriculum of the elementary schools was based on the notion of social utility – 'what is useful to teach the sons and daughters of the working classes'. Thus an emphasis on basic skill competence dominated the infant classes' timetables. Parents were required to pay fees of from a penny to two pence a week. Children from the age of 3 could be taken into schools and the 'babies' rooms' continued to offer training in alphabet recitation, picture recognition and marching to music. The young children of the middle classes were educated at home by tutors or in private schools. In the late nineteenth century it was estimated that only 41 per cent of working-class children aged 6 to 10 attended grant-aided elementary schools (NEU 1870: 6). In 1870 School Boards were established as was the principle that new schools should be financed by a combination of low fees, local rates and central government funding, while the voluntary schools funded by the church ran alongside this provision. Upon this principle local authority primary schools and church schools still coexist today. An Act of 1876 enforced compulsory school attendance on children over 5. In 1891 it was determined that parents could demand free education for their children. In 1893 the employment age for children was raised to 11 and in 1918 the statutory school leaving age was raised to 14. The rigid government control over the elementary school curriculum was gradually eased by a series of Revised Codes. In 1926 central control over the curriculum was finally lifted. From then on elementary school teachers were 'guided ' by a handbook of suggestions rather than constrained by a set of regulations. It is sometimes hard to believe that all this was happening within living memory and ironic to realize that sixty years later, by the terms of the Education Reform Act 1988, we have come full circle back to a centrally controlled National Curriculum.

The 1930s saw an expansion of nursery education in Britain with pioneering work by the McMillan sisters and Susan Isaacs (to which we shall return on pp. 13–15). It was the Hadow Reports of 1931 and 1933 (Board of Education) that marked the beginnings of the concept of 'primary education'. In the first report it was recommended that infants (3–7) and juniors (7–11) should be taught separately but with close liaison between the two sectors and that 'the curriculum is to be thought of in terms of activity and experience rather than of knowledge to be acquired and facts to be stored'. The curriculum was considered under three broad headings: natural activities (including play), expressive training (including handwork), and formal instruction in the 3Rs. It was recommended that the teaching of reading should begin at 6.

The 1933 report recommended that there should be special facilities – premises and staffing ratios – for very young children in primary schools. The purpose of nursery 'training' should be to assist the unfolding of the child's natural powers. Its functions should be educational but the methods recommended were for children to be encouraged to observe, handle objects and make things, working in small groups in order to learn from their own actions. Class instruction was discouraged.

In the Education Act 1944 infant education was subsumed into primary education. The Act marked fundamental changes in attitudes towards an entitlement to education for all. This was partly the result of the feeling that since everybody had contributed to the war effort then everybody was rightful heir to a welfare state which guaranteed a minimum standard of health, education and economic status regardless of social class. The statutory school starting age was to remain at 5, but there was an obligation for local authorities to provide nursery classes. Most children started school in the term after their fifth birthday; thus an accident of birth could determine whether a child spent between six and nine terms in infant schooling. Once inside the school most 5-year-olds would find a diet of look and say reading, phonics, basic computation, copy writing and occasional Friday afternoon play activities.

Progressive schools were pushing ahead with innovations such as integrated days – where a number of curriculum activities would be going on simultaneously with children working through tasks at their own pace – and vertical grouping arrangements – where children were taught in mixed age groups. But as with many of the shifts in policy we have identified so far, the effects of changes in other phases of education filtered down into infant schools. The school leaving age was to be raised to 16, and in order to assist the processes of secondary reorganization, the Education Act 1964 made it possible for LEAs to vary the age of transfer of pupils from one stage of schooling to the next. This legislation paved the way for the recommendations of the Plowden Report 1967 (CACE 1967) that young children would be best served by an educational system which provided nursery education for all whose parents wished for it, first schools for children from 5 to 8, and middle schools for 8–12-year-olds. By 1975 there were 2,093 first schools spread amongst 48 LEAs. Nevertheless most children aged 5 to 8 in the UK are educated in infant schools for ages 5 to 7, or primary schools for ages 5 to 11. It is also clear that despite the official school starting age of 5, more and more children are entering their first school at 4, an issue which will be addressed later.

The Plowden Report marked a great upsurge of confidence in the child-centred approach to education defined by Hadow in the 1930s. The most famous passage from Plowden is still used as the clarion call of the so-called Progressive movement in primary education:

> at the heart of the education process lies the child. No advances in policy, no acquisitions of new equipment have their desired effect unless they are in harmony with the nature of the child, unless they are fundamentally acceptable to him.
>
> (CACE 1967: para 9)

There was an underlying belief in education as a good thing in itself, part of a liberal view of the entitlement of the British public to a publicly funded education system.

Running alongside the concept of 'entitlement' of all children to a state education was a growing concern about the effects of 'social deprivation': of low income, poor housing, racism. In infant and nursery schools in the 1960s and early 1970s there was a naive belief that compensatory education would serve to combat the known effects of social disadvantage on children's educational achievements. In the inner cities, money was pumped into an expansion of nursery classes attached to infant schools through the Urban Aid programmes. A major concern was to raise the level of language competence of working-class children. Plenty of Peabody Language Kits, a highly structured language teaching programme complete with plastic fruit for 'real' first-hand learning experiences, were shipped across from the USA to provide opportunities for young children to have structured language teaching sessions. However, it soon became apparent that in order for the programmes to have any real and lasting effect on the children, it was essential to involve parents in what was going on at school. These home/school initiatives were followed up by extensive programmes of involving parents in listening to children reading (see e.g. J. Tizard *et al.* 1982; Topping 1984; 1985). The involvement of parents in the governing bodies of schools also became a political issue. In 1977 the Taylor Report (DES 1977a) recommended that parents should make up one-quarter of the governing bodies of schools. The recommendation was finally implemented in Sections 1 to 4 of the Education Act (2) 1986, which now form the basis of the new regulations for the composition of governing bodies.

Everything seemed possible in the 1960s. There was a genuine optimism about the role of education in the development of both the individual and the society within which the individual would flourish. But the student demonstrations in the late 1960s in Paris and in the British universities – Essex, the London School of Economics, and Leeds – rocked the Establishment. The babies reared under the edicts of Benjamin Spock (1970), whose child-rearing manual was on the shelf of countless parents of the 1950s and 1960s, and in the so-called progressive classrooms of the Plowden era, had turned into rebellious, long-haired, young adults refusing to submit to adult authority.

Inevitably a reaction set in against Progressive Education. In 1969 the first right-wing Black Paper appeared (see Cox and Dyson 1971) criticizing the supposed *laissez-faire* attitude of schools towards basic skill teaching and maintaining that standards of education were declining. In 1975 a junior school in Islington, the William Tyndale school, was the subject of a government inquiry which resulted in the publication of the Auld Report (Auld 1976). The headteacher, Terry Ellis, and the deputy headteacher, Brian Haddow, were criticized for their liberal attitudes towards allowing children to choose their own ways of working to the point where children in the school became 'bored and listless'. At the same time a research project by Neville Bennett (Bennett 1976), into the effectiveness of thirty-seven primary teachers designated as formal or informal in their teaching styles, gave the superficial impression that pupils achieved 'better' results in schools with formal teachers. In fact the *most* successful teacher in the study was an informal teacher who set clear goals and was well organized in her style of working in the classroom. The press chose to take a simplistic view of the results and used them to hammer the cause of progressivism.

This kind of public anxiety was reflected in 1976 in a speech by the then Prime Minister, James Callaghan, at Ruskin College. It is worth quoting extracts from this important landmark of a speech, delivered by a Labour politician, which heralded the educational policy changes of Thatcherism in the 1980s. He argued that

> parents, teachers, learned and professional bodies, representatives of higher education and both sides of industry, together with the Government, all have an important part to play in formulating and expressing the purpose of education and the standards that we need.

Callaghan went on to identify the complaints of employers that 'new recruits from the schools sometimes do not have the basic tools to do the job that is required'. He also talked in guarded terms about

> the unease felt by parents and teachers about the new informal methods of teaching which seem to produce excellent results when they are in well-qualified hands but are much more dubious in their effects when they are not.

He concluded

> There is a challenge to us all in these days and the challenge in education is to examine its priorities and to secure as high efficiency as you can by the skilful use of £6 billion of existing resources. Let me repeat some of the fields that need study because they cause concern. There are the methods and aims of informal instruction. The strong case for the

so-called core curriculum of basic knowledge. What is the proper way of monitoring the use of resources in order to maintain a proper national standard of performance? What is the role of the inspectorate in relation to national standards and their maintenance? And there is a need to improve relations between industry and education.

(Reported in the *Times Educational Supplement* 22 October 1976)

Other research into primary classrooms in the 1970s did not report the kind of mayhem that the press ascribed to 'progressive' state schooling. The ORACLE project based at Leicester University found little evidence in the junior classrooms studied over a three-year period to substantiate 'the claim that anarchy and confusion prevail in primary school classrooms' (Galton *et al.* 1980: 156). An HMI survey of primary schools published in 1978 actually warned teachers against an over-emphasis on basic skill teaching.

Anxiety is sometimes expressed that maintaining a wide curriculum in primary schools may be possible only at the expense of the essential, elementary skills of reading, writing and mathematics. The evidence from the HMI survey of primary education in England does not bear out this anxiety. A broad curriculum can include many opportunities for the application and practice of the skills of reading, writing and calculating. It should be planned to include them, and every opportunity should then be taken to improve children's abilities in these essential skills.

(DES 1978a: 12)

Nevertheless the call for accountability signalled by the Ruskin College speech escalated into a full-bloodied yell. The DES issued Circular 14/77 (DES 1977b) asking all local authorities to answer questions about the arrangements they had for curricular delivery in schools. In a report on the responses published in 1979 it was suggested that 'not all authorities have a clear view of the desirable structure of the school curriculum, especially the core elements'. The belief was expressed that the Secretaries of State 'should seek to give a lead in the process of reaching a national consensus on a desirable framework for the curriculum and consider the development of such a framework a priority for the education service' (DES 1979: 6). 'The secret garden' of the curriculum referred to by the then Conservative Minister of Education, Sir David Eccles, in a debate in the House of Commons in 1960 (reported in Manzer 1970) where anybody other than teachers 'who attempted to trespass there were very firmly warned off' was about to be invaded. Moreover, it became clear that the separation of infant, junior/middle and secondary schools curricula was to be discouraged. Documents pouring from the DES during the 1980s focused on curriculum matters from 5 to 16, for example *The School Curriculum* (DES 1981), *The Curriculum from 5 to 16* (DES 1985b) and *Educational Reform: Government Proposals for Schools* (DES 1987). The curriculum was seen very much as a continuum: 'the 5–16 curriculum needs to be constructed and delivered as a continuous and coherent whole, in which the primary phase prepares for the secondary phase, and the latter builds on the former' (DES 1985b: para 65).

With unemployment running at high levels and public disagreements between the Labour Party and the unions, the stage was set for a landslide electoral defeat. In 1979 Margaret Thatcher began a long reign during the course of which successive Secretaries of State for Education wielded increasing power over every aspect of education. The first tentative moves towards centralized control escalated into the vast changes in the traditions of Welsh and English primary education heralded by the 'Great' Education Reform Bill of 1988. Whether infant teachers liked it or not they were thrust into the maelstrom of educational change legislated for within the terms of the Education Reform Act 1988 (NCC/WO 1989a), and into the mainstream of debate about curriculum content, assessment, changes in governing bodies and local financial management. Indeed infant schools became the focus of particular attention when the National Curriculum was introduced to 5-year-olds first in September 1989, with the first round of assessment of the targets of attainment being practised on those children in the summer term of 1991 when they were aged 7.

Ideologies

In trying to understand infant and first schools as they are now it is also essential to be aware of the history of ideas which have influenced the ideologies of infant teachers. As Nan Whitbread (1972) points out, the ideologies of nursery and infant teachers have been meshed together by historical events. Though there are vociferous opponents in both 'camps' to moves to lump nursery and infant education together as Early Years Education, in fact the increasing emphasis on nursery education being provided in classes or units attached to infant or primary schools, the closure of separate nursery schools and the huge increase in 4-year-olds being admitted into reception classes have all conspired to force nursery and infant teachers to work alongside each other. The closure of nursery schools has been justified on the grounds that it is better for the children and their parents to have an 'all through' notion of the first few years in school and that nursery classes are therefore preferable. This notion is a reflection of the current emphasis on continuity and progression within the National Curriculum 5 to 16. The admission of 4-year-olds into the reception classes of primary schools has been justified on the grounds that they are better off with an early start to school. The more likely reasons are that these policy changes have been *ad hoc* responses to financial constraints and have resulted in nursery education on the cheap for many young children.

There is evidence from the longitudinal Child Health and Education Study at Bristol (Osborn and Milbank 1987) that children who have experienced nursery education in nursery schools achieved higher scores on a range of tests of competence in language, numeracy and verbal reasoning when tested at age 5 and age 10 than those who have attended nursery classes (though in fact the best results were achieved by those children who had attended small home-based playgroups!). One explanation of these results may be that nursery schools are more likely to be staffed by teachers with nursery education training – rarely the case with nursery classes – and that children at nursery schools are therefore given a better start to their schooling. However, the social contexts in which parents will travel some distance to take their children to nursery schools out of a belief in their value, and the data on home-based playgroups, indicate that parental attitudes and circumstances in the study affected the children's long-term gains in educational achievement. Nevertheless there is indisputable evidence of the inadequate staffing, resources and curriculum provision being offered to many of the 4-year-olds in reception classes (Cleave *et al*. 1982; NFER/SCDC 1987; N. Bennett and Kell 1989) in comparison with the legal requirements of staffing and resourcing of the nursery provision to which this age group is entitled.

Whatever the vagaries in the provision and funding of the education of young children, infant classrooms sit uneasily between ideologies shared with their nursery colleagues and those of their primary class teacher colleagues. Lesley Webb wrote, 'One must not overlook or underestimate the existence of the "common law" of English nursery education, nor assume that because it is often unformulated and too rarely subjected to analysis its writs no longer run' (Webb 1974: 4). Robin Alexander has described the origins of primary teachers' ideology of child-centredness (Alexander 1984: 15). Yet many infant school students and indeed practising teachers perpetuate practices derived from these received ideas without ever recognizing the origins of their beliefs or in fact questioning the validity of what they habitually do. Why do we claim to base the curriculum of young children on play activities? Why do we have house corners? Why do we send children out to play for up to two hours a day on to freezing, barren school playgrounds? Why do we have reading schemes, unifix cubes, Lego or jigsaws? Why are we so nervous about 'teaching' creative activities or handwriting? Why do we have those mysteriously misnamed 'choosing times'? In order to grapple with these kinds of questions we need to review some of the major influences on beliefs about nursery and primary education, since the two traditions flow into infant classrooms like currents in a tidal estuary.

Froebel

It is to Froebel (1782–1852) that we owe the legacy of valuing play to the point of what Dearden (1968) describes as eulogizing it. Froebel had an almost mystical belief in the value of spontaneous play, 'the highest level of child development'. (Froebel 1826: para 30). He wrote 'Play at this time is not trivial, it is highly serious and of deep significance'. Dearden quotes the whimsical extract from Rousseau's *Emile (Book 2)* which encapsulates the notion of school learning as being the antithesis of pleasure:

> The hour strikes, the scene is changed. All of a sudden his eye grows dim, his mirth is fled. Farewell mirth, farewell untrammelled sports in which he delighted. A stern, angry man takes him by the hand, saying gravely, 'Come with me, sir', and he is led away. As they are entering the room, I catch a glimpse of books. . . . The poor child allows himself to be dragged away; he casts a sorrowful look on all about him, and departs in silence, his eyes swollen with tears he dare not shed, and his heart bursting with the sighs he dare not utter.
>
> (Quoted in Dearden, 1968: 94)

Play has been defined as a 'non-serious' activity and an activity which is 'spontaneous and self-generated' (Lowenfeld 1935: 37) but this definition sits uneasily alongside Froebel's more austere version of learning through play. Froebel expected that children should play with the Gifts which made up the resources for the key Occupations for learning in a carefully prescribed manner. It is fascinating to note that when the Occupations were done by rote in the tiered galleries of the monitorial schools, the purpose was defined as 'to train hand and eye', an appropriate technical skill for future artisans. More fascinating still is the repetition of history in the choice of Technology as the first foundation subject of the National Curriculum to be introduced to 5-year-olds in 1990 in the belief that this will provide a firm basis for the supply of skilled technicians for the work-force of the twenty-first century! The legacy of Froebel's belief that practical craft work – making up geometric designs with coloured wooden squares and triangles, paper-folding and weaving, stick-laying and construction, sewing and embroidery – leading to sensory and language training should be central features of the school curriculum is still in evidence in infant classrooms. Think about the table-top toys that start many infant children's daily dose of education, and the number of student school practice topics based on 'The Senses'.

Montessori

Maria Montessori (1870–1952) was a doctor and psychologist. Her handbook *The Montessori Method* was first published in English in 1914, in the USA, and the first edition of 5,000 copies sold out within four days. Maria Montessori had pioneered her *Casa dei Bambini* (Children's House) in the slums of Rome. It is worth quoting an extract from the handbook to get the full flavour of the revolutionary learning environment Montessori prescribed for young children:

> The 'Children's House' . . . ought to be a real house; that is to say, a set of rooms with a garden of which the children are the masters. A garden

which contains shelters is ideal, because the children can play or sleep under them, and can also bring their tables out to work and dine. In this way they may live almost entirely in the open air, and are protected at the same time from rain and sun.

The central and principal room of the building, often also the only room at the disposal of the children, is the room for 'intellectual work'. To this central room can be added other smaller rooms according to the means and opportunities of the place: for example a bathroom, a dining-room, a little parlor or common room, a room for manual work, a gymnasium and rest-room.

The special characteristics of the equipment of these houses is that it is adapted for children and not adults. They contain not only didactic material specially fitted for the intellectual development of the child, but also complete equipment for the management of the miniature family. The furniture is light so that the children can move it about, and it is painted in some light color so that the children can wash it with soap and water. There are low tables of various shapes and sizes – square, rectangular and round, large and small. The rectangular shape is the most common as two or more children can work at it together. The seats are small wooden chairs, but there are also small wicker armchairs and sofas.

In the working-room there are two indispensable pieces of furniture. One of these is a very long cupboard with large doors. It is very low so that a small child can set on the top of it small objects such as mats, flowers etc. Inside this cupboard is kept the didactic material which is the common property of all the children.

The other is a chest of drawers containing two or three columns of little drawers, each of which has a bright handle (or a handle of some colour to contrast with the background) and a small card with a name upon it. Every child has his own drawer, in which to put things belonging to him.

(Montessori 1972: 37–9)

There are so many elements here of an idealized infant classroom environment that it makes one smile inwardly to recognize how firmly Montessori still has a hold over us. Montessori believed that children should learn in an environment which replicated their home lives but to child-size scale: 'this method seeks to give all this to the child in reality – making him an actor in a living scene' (Montessori 1972: 47).

Children were to spend their days cooking, cleaning, and playing outside in the garden. In this sense, our house corners are a pale imitation of Montessori's intentions. It is also interesting that the English tradition of nursery education, with a much greater emphasis on the value of fantasy play, renamed the Children's House the Wendy House of J. M. Barrie's *Peter Pan* (Barrie 1915) and now of course those concerned with gender issues in early years education have insisted that boys should not feel excluded from domesticity by Wendy's ownership and so it has been renamed again to the gender neutral label 'the house corner'.

In the room designated for 'intellectual work', children would be expected to select from particular shelves, according to their levels of competence, sets of the didactic materials – carefully prescribed sets of wooden rods, sticks, cubes, insets (we still have an obsession with wooden rather than plastic aids for learning in infant classrooms!), card alphabets and numbers, lacing and buttoning exercises, bells, etc. – often bringing small mats to table tops or the floor so that they could frame a space for their work with the apparatus. The role of the teacher was simply to set up the child-centred learning environment and to observe the children's progress through the set procedures defined by the structured apparatus – 'the teacher in our method is more of an observer than a teacher, therefore this is what the teacher must know, how to observe'.

> It is necessary for the teacher to guide the child without letting him feel her presence too much, so that she may be always ready to supply the desired help, but may never be the obstacle between the child and his experience. . . . There is no need for intervention. 'Wait while observing.' That is the motto for the educator.
>
> (Montessori 1972: 131–2)

The legacy of not intervening in the child's personal voyage of discovery, which was to be developed by John Dewey, remains as a strong force within the ideologies of infant teachers, and is a theme which will be explored in some detail later in this book.

Steiner

Rudolf Steiner's (1861–1925) vision of education was to help each person to find his or her right place in life and to fulfil a personal destiny. He believed in the absolute supremacy of the individual over the demands of the institution or state. He believed that 'There are three effective agents in education: compulsion, ambition and love. We do without the first two' (Steiner 1926). He saw teachers as enablers or creators who would stay with one class, at least for a two-hour 'main lesson' which starts each day, throughout their schooling.

The Steiner curriculum is divided into three stages: the kindergarten from age 4 to 6 when children develop through practical experiences and imitation; the second stage from 6 to 14 when the emphasis is on imagination and feeling and the third stage from 14 to 18 when children are considered to be ready for intellectual abstraction and analysis. The teaching methods he pioneered are almost ritualistic – a great deal of oral work woven through with storying, drama, music, poetry, sewing, and a stylized movement to speech and music called Eurithmy. Stages at which children are ready to tackle formal academic work are strictly laid down. Children aged 6 and 7 are introduced to the alphabet by stories and pictures about individual letters, but children are not expected to learn to read, for example, until their eighth year.

The schools are staffed by a non-hierarchical 'republic of teachers', often on very low wages. Steiner schools sprang up in the UK between the 1960s and the 1980s as 'alternative schools' to the state primary system. Steiner has come to be called the 'guru of the Greens', but apart from his appeal to the so-called hippy parents who opt for Steiner schooling for their children, we have all retained from Guru Steiner the intense concern for the individual child in the English tradition of early education, the slightly fey approach of some infant teachers to the 'mystery and wonder' of childhood and the Plowdenesque notion that 'at the heart of education lies the child'. When Pat Ashton and colleagues (1975) asked primary teachers to rank their aims for education, of the seventy-two aims listed in her study, six of the top eight were to do with personal and social development and the sixth was, in fact, 'The child should be an individual developing in his [sic] own way.'

McMillan

The formidable McMillan sisters, Margaret (1860–1931) and Rachel (1859–1917), worked in Bradford and London to establish 'open air' nursery schools. The open verandahs down one side of each classroom were designed to stop the spread of TB, ear, eye and throat infections. Without antibiotics these infections could cause real distress amongst young children. Many head-teachers in inner city schools in the 1970s and 1980s have waited in exasperation for these draughty verandahs to be closed in to make extra corridor or storage space. The McMillans worked directly from the philanthropic tradition of the late nineteenth century. Margaret was openly political, campaigning within the traditions of the Independent Labour Party in the 1920s, in her demands for schools to cater for the physical and social needs of slum children. Children were seen to need physical nurturing – well-scrubbed bodies, a wholesome diet, regular medical inspections – before they might be subjected to intellectual work. Given the physical conditions of inner city life in the 1920s, the McMillans had their priorities right; but the obsession with fresh air and exercise *per se* as intrinsically good for children can still dominate much of the infant school day. In fact it is hard to know how else we could justify the percentage of the school day which is written off as 'playing out', often on uncompromisingly bare tarmac school yards with no attention whatsoever paid to the quality of play the children are experiencing.

In *Education Through Imagination* (1923) Margaret McMillan wrote 'To educate the hand and to safeguard the speech impulse: that is perhaps the main work – of a formal kind – of the nursery school'. The sisters were also strongly influenced by William Morris and John Ruskin's writing and believed in the importance of aesthetics in the curriculum. They believed in the need for 'a new order of workman' capable of exercising 'enterprise, initiative – plus what is learned – Imagination'. Teaching was organized into small groups – six in a group for children under 5 and twelve for 5 pluses – with a young girl 'helper' working with the children, but all under the direction of a trained teacher. There was a benign, domestic and essentially maternal atmosphere in the classrooms.

Isaacs

Later Susan Isaacs (1885–1948) was to explore the intellectual growth of young children from her base at the Malting House School in Cambridge. She worked in a different tradition from the socialist reforming zeal of the McMillan sisters. The Malting House School was financed by a wealthy business man, Geoffrey Pike, and the children, aged between 2½ and 9 years, were well-heeled and often exceptionally bright. Susan Isaacs devoted much of her research into the minds of young children towards those with psychological problems. She was strongly influenced by Melanie Klein's (Klein 1949) work on Freudian theories of children's emotional and social development. She was concerned that the teacher should develop 'true scientific understanding' of young children's learning. Isaacs wrote in her pamphlet on *The Educational Value of the Nursery School*

> Children need not only the right play-material, but skilled help in their own efforts to learn and understand, and in their struggles with their anti-social impulses. To know what is the right word to say to the shy or inhibited child, the angry and destructive child, to have the right answer ready to an intellectual problem, to see when to introduce the child to a new piece of number apparatus, to understand when to interfere and when to leave alone, when to check defiance or stop a quarrel, and when to allow the child to solve his own problem, when to encourage and when to remain silent, is not a wisdom that comes simply by nature. Certainly it rests upon natural qualities. The nursery school teacher no less than the mother must have love and sympathy, natural insight and the patience to learn; but children need more than this in their struggles with the many problems we have glimpsed. They need true scientific under-standing as well as mother-wit and mother-love.
>
> (Isaacs 1948: 72)

Susan Isaacs used close and systematic observations of children engaged in problem-solving activities in normal nursery school settings, rather than in laboratory conditions, to develop her understanding of children's intellectual growth. Of all the early pioneers her stance probably will sit most comfortably alongside the ideologies of many infant teachers in the 1990s. She described how she viewed the function of nursery education:

> The children are free to explore and experiment with the physical world, the way things are made, the fashion in which they break and burn, the

properties of water and gas and electric light, the rain, sunshine, the mud and the frost. They are free to create either by fantasy or imaginative play or by real handling of clay and wood and bricks. The teacher is there to meet this free enquiry and activity by his skill in bringing together the material and the situations which may give children the means of answering their own questions about the world.

(reported in van der Eycken and Turner 1969: 39)

It is significant that Susan Isaacs saw the role of the teacher as not only supportive but also interventionist. The teacher must 'have the right answer ready for an intellectual problem' and is there to 'meet' the children's free enquiry and activity with careful structuring of learning experiences and situations. Though she valued observation of young children as highly as Maria Montessori and appreciated the values of the maternal nurturing role, she saw the role of the teacher as far more specialized, positive and active in promoting the child's learning.

Conflicting imperatives

Two separate strands of theorizing began to dominate educational publications in the twentieth century of interest to infant teachers. The developmental psychological tradition focused on the stages through which children's learning progressed. Sociological studies of classrooms focused on the contextual influences on children's progress in schools. These theories will be set against the third imperative influencing infant classrooms, the instrumental view of early years education inherited from the Elementary Schools.

The developmental psychological tradition

The Froebelian naturalist developmental tradition argued that the teacher's role was to set up a learning environment where children might learn through first-hand experiences. The influence of psychology, particularly of the theories of Jean Piaget (which will be explored in Chapter 2), was powerful. Children were expected to move through defined stages of learning towards maturity of thought.

The kinds of principles which underpinned the developmental psychological model applied to professional practice are exemplified in the following list of 'generalizations' which appear in a book emanating from the Froebel Institute as late as 1969 (Brearley *et al.* 1969). The group of authors was chaired by Molly Brearley:

1 Children are unique persons and their individuality is to be acknowledged and respected.
2 Each person constructs his own mind as a result of interaction with things

and people in his environment, and interaction between his own inner experiences.

3 Learning is continuous and knowledge cumulative.

4 The concept of 'stages' in intellectual development is useful in helping to understand some distinguishable phases of development in a child's thought.

5 Children encouraged in co-operative efforts with other children and with teachers will collaborate in the search for and the sharing of knowledge.

6 The mental processes involved in the search for knowledge and understanding contain their own self-expanding and extending propulsion.

(Brearley *et al.* 1969: 159)

Each child was to be seen as an 'individual' in the classroom. The following manifesto of a primary teacher, reported by Coe (1966), typifies this belief:

I know all my children as individuals. Of course there are times when we come together and share activities like music making, drama or perhaps just quietly listening to a story. But in basic work I give twenty different lessons. The children work individually, each at their own pace, and I circulate among them, helping, guiding and correcting. Always I have the particular need of the child in mind. Sometimes the children work in groups helping each other. Class lessons? They just wouldn't work. . . . I never teach a class. I teach children.

(Coe 1966: 77)

The ideology of 'liberal romanticism' (Richards 1982) which starts from the individual child when developing educational principles and sees the teacher as working 'alongside' the child was best demonstrated in the 1960s and 1970s in the village schools of Oxfordshire or in Leicestershire or the former West Riding of Yorkshire. These geographical clusters of 'progressivism' in primary schools were associated with charismatic characters like Robin Tanner, Alec Clegg or Sybil Marshall. Sybil Marshall's book *An Experiment in Education* (published in 1963) still reads as an inspirational document and its breathless enthusiasm for educating children explains the profound influence those great educators had on a generation of teachers and children:

Education must have an end in view, for it is not an end in itself. The end can only be the knowledge of what it means really to live, and the wisdom to accept and make the most of what life offers each individual person.

(Marshall 1963: 170)

Many infant teachers today would claim to espouse such an ideology.

Classroom 'realities' – the sociologists' views

However, in the 1970s a more rigorously analytical study of infant school · practice from a predominantly 'left-wing' political standpoint began to prevail as issues of inequality in education were explored by researchers. Research studies like Sharp and Green's seminal sociological analysis of infant classrooms, *Education and Social Control: a Study in Progressive Primary Education* (1975) and King's *All Things Bright and Beautiful? A Sociological Study of Infants' Classrooms* (1978) challenged the ideology of 'liberal romanticism'. The researchers' frameworks of reference were poles apart from those of infant school teachers and they confidently offered evidence that infant teachers were unable to act in classrooms in the way their rhetoric *claimed* that they were acting. For example in the classrooms studied by Sharp and Green and by King children were not treated as individuals, nor given free choice of activities, nor allowed to develop at their own pace. There was evidence also that the teachers' typifications of pupils affected the way they responded to different groups of children within their classes, and that teacher responses to children and their expectations of them had tangible effects on pupil progress in schooling. These findings will be discussed later in this book in some detail since they represent some of the first attempts to collect evidence of the 'realities' rather than the 'rhetoric' of English infant school practice.

Teaching the basics – the elementary school tradition

The 'realities' were in fact strongly influenced by the alternative major ideology stemming from the elementary school tradition which determines the beliefs of infant school teachers: the utilitarian view that education is about introducing children to the basic skills which will make them into useful and productive citizens and workers. Basic skills are largely interpreted as numeracy and literacy and, above all in infant schools, as learning to read. In these 'basics' the style of instruction in infant classrooms has continued to be largely didactic, though often the didacticism is presented in the 'soft' form of individualized, group or structured scheme-based teaching. The model of instruction implicit in the elementary school ideology implies an interventionist stance, rather than the non-interventionist role of the teacher implicit in a child-centred model of infant education. Evidence from recent research studies of infant classrooms indicates that it is basic skills teaching that continues to occupy most teacher and indeed pupil time (DES 1982a; Bennett N. *et al*. 1984; Tizard *et al*. 1988).

In one sense, infant teachers are simply responding to the demands of society, or more specifically of parents, to get on with 'proper' schooling. On the whole parents favour the old elementary school tradition of instruction in the 3Rs – reading, writing and arithmetic. Froebel, Steiner, Montessori, and Discovery Learning are seen by the majority of parents as the province of a minority of intellectuals and middle-class romantic liberals who mostly have a shrewd knowledge of how to work the education system anyway. 'Normal' parents are suspicious of learning through play. What is more, most local education authorities and in-school tests at infant stages have been in literacy and numeracy, above all in reading, and infant teachers have been answerable to those test results. Ironically, though infant teachers are hostile towards the notion of testing children on a National Curriculum at the age of 7 as recommended by the Task Group on Assessment and Testing in Schools (DES 1988a), if this model is finally put into practice, the pressure on infant teachers to pay real rather than rhetorical attention to practical experiential learning may become greater than ever before. The report recommended that testing at 7 should be cross-curricular and based on 'normal' infant classroom practice, which was assumed to include group work, a schematic approach to curriculum planning and practical learning activities. Piloting of Standard Assessment Tasks based on those principles in the Summer of 1990, proved how complex this approach to testing is. Nevertheless it is salutory to remind ourselves that testing in the elementary school system, upon which payment by results was based, was also first implemented in Standard 1, the 7-year-olds' class, in 1862. Perhaps infant teachers are wise to be cautious about the long-term use to which centrally imposed test results might be put.

It must be pointed out that teachers working in inner cities have found the quintessentially English village school philosophies, inherited from Sybil Marshall, Alec Clegg and Robin Tanner, difficult to implement in the very different contexts of strife-riven inner city life. The premise that all children *want* to learn does not always seem to hold in the middle of Hulme, Toxteth or

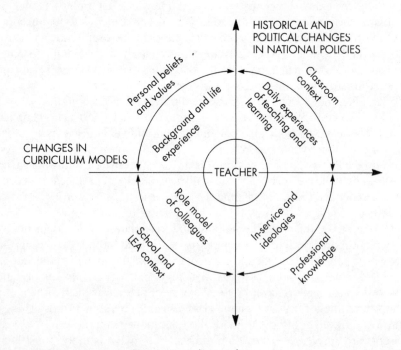

Figure 1   Conflicting influences on the teacher

Newham! However, since this model has often been held up as 'The Ideal' during their training, teachers have been made to feel guilty that they have fallen short of such lofty aspirations. Hence the gap between the rhetoric and the reality exposed by the research of Sharp and Green and King has remained a constant feature of infant school life.

Thus infant teachers in the 1990s find themselves caught between the relentless currents of child-centred progressivism and utilitarian demands to teach the basic skills. Marooned in such an uncomfortable position, it will not be surprising if they feel vulnerable and confused as to how they should set about reaching the shore. Their uncertainty has been further compounded by legislation which prescribes National Curriculum core and foundation subject content and assessment procedures for 5–7-year-olds mainly on the basis of a secondary school curriculum system backed down into infant classrooms.

The complex working context in which teachers find themselves is perhaps best summarized in Figure 1.

On one axis education is inevitably caught up in the processes of changes in the national priorities and policies of whichever political group currently wields the most power. On the other arm of the axis, the ideologies of local and national hierarchies in educational policy-making and administration determine the curriculum models imposed upon schools. At times a set of political interests may be at odds with a conflicting set of educational policies determined by strong vested interests within the education profession. The teacher is buffeted backwards and forwards along the two axes by the power of these external forces.

But I believe that the power of the forces represented within the four enclosing segments of Figure 1 upon the teacher is *much* stronger than the pressure exerted upon them from outside the school system. This power is largely unrecognized by both politicians and policy-makers. In the course of the argument within the book, each of these four interrelated areas of influence acting upon the teacher – their daily classroom context, their professional knowledge, the role model of colleagues, and teachers' personal beliefs and values – will be examined.

In this complex, demanding and ever-changing climate, infant teachers are struggling to find their way. The hope is that subsequent chapters of this book, in trying to clarify issues related to young children's learning, the role of the teacher of young children and the infant school curriculum, will support them in their struggle and give due recognition to their considerable and underrated professional expertise.

2

Children learning

All teachers are exposed to some aspects of psychology during initial training. However, it is clear that infant teachers are no exceptions in finding it difficult to make the links between what Edgar Stones (1984) has described as 'galloping through the gurus' and the hectic realities of trying to understand how the young children in their classrooms learn. In other words the 'knowledge' of psychology courses offered to teachers at initial or in-service level is not transferred easily by teachers to their day-to-day practices. Why should this be so?

In the first place, the kind of psychology offered to teachers has not on the whole been drawn from the realities that they recognize. Traditionally for most teachers in post now, the dominant models offered in educational psychology courses have been Behaviourism, particularly B. F. Skinner (1974), and the radically different model of Developmental Psychology proposed by Jean Piaget (Piaget 1971). The behaviourist psychologists have been presented as viewing the child as a *tabula rasa* at birth. The child learns by passively reacting to stimuli and to the reinforcements which the environment or people within that environment provide. Students in training have been offered accounts of rats and pigeons being put through various uncomfortable experiences as the basis for demonstrations of behaviourist theory in action. Naturally they have found the insights gained from the study of the hapless creatures' responses to the levers, mazes, buzzers and food dispensers in these experiments difficult to transfer to their experiences with children in classrooms! At the other extreme, the Piagetian view has presented the child as actively constructing his or her own thinking by acting upon the physical and social environment. All children were seen to develop through a series of clearly defined stages towards logical thinking. Most research evidence offered in support of the developmental psychology model was drawn from observations of children in home or laboratory conditions. Again, teachers have found it difficult to make useful links between the model and their daily work with children in classrooms.

It seems that psychological theories have either not been explained with sufficient clarity to engage the interest and commitment of the teaching profession – there is a great deal of jargon to plough through – or the implications for classrooms have not been clearly defined, or the theories offered have been so contradictory that teachers have simply given up in exasperation and rejected the whole package (see Barrow 1984).

Bruner (1980) wrote, 'It is only when research helps one to see with one's own eyes that it gets beneath the skin': this highlights a second significant issue. It is only recently that teachers of young children have begun to engage in research and higher degree work in their own right. Even when it was glaringly obvious that the 'knowledge' offered on conventional educational psychology courses was not transferable to their life in classrooms, teachers were themselves reluctant to challenge the conventional wisdom offered to them by the discipline of psychology. Particularly in the field of early years education, a predominantly female work-force has been socialized by the kinds of social processes of parental aspirations, careers advice at school and patterns of male-dominated promotion in primary education (see De Lyon and Migniuolo 1989) into low expectations of their own academic capabilities and the sense that somebody up there knew better than them. It is sobering to realize that equal pay for women teachers was fully implemented only in 1961! Hence teachers actually rank knowledge of child development and psychology high on their list of what 'knowledge' is useful to teachers despite their obvious difficulties in making use of this expertise.

What happened then was that teachers, because of misplaced deference towards the 'gurus' of psychology, adopted basic psychological frameworks for talking about their classroom practices, what Walkerdine (1985) calls 'the conceptualizations which form the bedrock of modern practices', without rigorously analysing the underlying theories. They express the conceptualizations in common-sense terms such as 'individualized learning', 'experience', 'readiness' and 'concepts'. In other words, they extract from the mass of 'knowledge' offered only those aspects of psychological theory that seem most relevant to their classroom practice. They simply convert the mysteries of psychological theories into classroom common sense and borrow from the psychologists some of the more accessible terms. In doing so they tend to use the terminology more as slogans than as tools for analysing the learning behaviours and processes of the pupils in their classrooms.

Drawing upon both psychological conceptualizations and the ideologies outlined in Chapter 1, most infant teachers would claim to subscribe to the following tenets about young children's learning:

1 Children develop in sequential stages from concrete to abstract levels of thinking.
2 A child must be 'ready' to move on to the next developmental stage and must not be forced to move to a higher level of cognitive functioning (e.g. in beginning to read, in recording numbers, in learning to conserve).
3 Children learn through first-hand experiences, particularly through play activities.
4 Children need to develop competence in language use to function effectively as school learners.
5 In social development children move from egocentrism to the ability to empathize with others.
6 Every child is an individual learning in his or her own unique way.

There is a new generation of researchers working hard to operate within the conceptual frameworks of teachers *and* a new generation of teachers who are determined to engage with and generate new ideas about children's learning. The six tenets will be examined in the light of some recent research which has attempted to bridge the gap between the 'disengaged' nature of psychological theorizing and the application of educational psychology to classroom realities. In each of the following six sections of the chapter the 'accepted' psychological thinking embedded within the tenets listed above will be reassessed in the light of new research and classroom evidence.

Children develop in sequential stages from concrete to abstract levels of thinking

This has been one of the most influential beliefs in infant classrooms since the 1950s. It has also caused teachers to underestimate the ability of young children to reason, and encouraged them to focus on what children cannot do 'yet' rather than to build on what they *can* do now. However, in the 1970s and 1980s, there was a radical change in emphasis to a much more open-ended and positive view of children's capabilities.

The Piagetian stages

Piaget labels the first eighteen months of a child's life the Sensori Motor phase; eighteen months to 4–5 years the stage of Intuitive Thought; and 4–5 to 7–8 years the stage of Concrete Operations. (See Brown and Desforges 1979, for a full critique of the Piagetian model of developmental stages.)

One of the most significant contributions towards helping teachers to reassess their understanding of the ways in which young children think and learn is Margaret Donaldson's book *Children's Minds* (Donaldson 1978). Using evidence gained from research studies based at the University of Edinburgh, she argued for a reinterpretation of the Piagetian view of children's cognitive development. Investigations were set up replicating some of the Piagetian tests but with important differences in the methodology of administering the tests to young children and in the nature of the tasks the children were set. The tasks were designed so that they made 'human sense' to the children. So, for example, the classic Piagetian 'Three Mountains Test' (see Piaget and Inhelder 1956) required children to say what they thought a doll could see when that doll was placed at various points around a model of three mountains distinguished from each other by features such as a house on top of one, snow on another, and a red cross on the third. Children were asked to choose from a set of ten pictures of the three mountains model taken from various angles, or to reconstruct a cardboard version of the model, to demonstrate what they thought the doll could see. Children under the age of 6 or 7 tended to choose the picture – or construct the model – which represented their own view of the three mountains from where they were sitting. This led Piaget to argue that the children were unable to 'decentre' from their own egocentric view of the world.

In a task devised by Martin Hughes for the Edinburgh studies, children were asked to explore the idea of whether a policeman, positioned at various points in a model of two intersecting walls, could see a boy who was hiding from him. After some exploratory talk, when the children were familiarized with the hypothetical situation of the boy hiding from the policeman and the function of the model in helping to explain the propositions, the children were then asked to hide the boy from two policemen, each of which were placed at the ends of two of the walls. With children between the ages of 3½ and 5 ninety per cent gave correct responses to the task. Hughes introduced a third policeman, complicated the arrangements of the intersecting walls still further, and still 3-year-olds achieved success rates of sixty per cent and 4-year-olds of ninety per cent on the tasks.

Donaldson argued that the children were able to demonstrate competence on the activities set up by Hughes because they were dealing with a situation to which they could relate. Most young children are familiar with the game of hide and seek and through television, or in some cases through family circumstances, they are also familiar with the notion of a baddie hiding from some figures of authority! Not many of our school population are familiar with viewing mountains from various strategic positions.

The point is that the motives and intentions of the characters [in Hughes' version of the experiment] are entirely comprehensible, even to a child of three. The task requires the child to act in ways which are in line with certain very basic human purposes and interactions (escape and pursuit) – it makes human sense. Thus it is not at all hard to convey to the child what he is supposed to do: he apprehends it instantly. It then turns out that neither is it hard for him to do it. In other words, in this context he shows none of the difficulty in 'decentring' which Piaget ascribes to him.

(Donaldson 1978: 24)

Another significant factor in the methodology adopted by the Edinburgh team was that the language that the adult researchers used in giving instructions was carefully structured and related to the purposes of the experimental activities so that the children were in no doubt as to what the tasks were about. With a clear sense of purpose, the children were thus able to demonstrate what they could do.

The team also explored young children's concept of conservation using a variety of activities. They discovered that children's performance on standard Piagetian tests designed to investigate conservation of number, volume, length, etc. was affected by their assumptions that adults must have a reason for rearranging rows of buttons or sticks or pouring water from one container to another. On standard Piagetian tests, the children's responses were therefore geared to answer adult questions with the replies they imagined the adults wanted to hear. When the agents of change in an experiment were seen by the children as less adult led and deliberate – almost as accidental events – children seemed to be freed from their sense that the adults questioning them knew what they were doing and therefore *required* certain responses. For example a classic Piagetian test of the child's ability to conserve numbers is to lay out two rows of the same number of buttons, ask children if there are the same number of buttons in each row, then rearrange one of the rows so that the buttons are spread further apart and repeat the question. In 'classic' Piagetian experiments, most young children appear to confuse the length of the row with the number of buttons, and respond that the longer row has more buttons. However, when James McGarrigle introduced the concept of a naughty teddy messing around with the buttons the children responded quite differently:

> McGarrigle found that this version of the task – where the transformation was ostensibly accidental – was dealt with much more successfully than the traditional version; many more children between the age of four and six 'conserved' – that is continued to say that the crucial attribute was the same.

(Donaldson 1978: 64)

The concept of sequential stages and schooling

Donaldson argues persuasively that we have been conditioned to under-estimate the rational powers of young children. She also argues that many of the activities we set young children in schools and the teaching strategies we adopt demonstrate the qualities of the Piagetian test situations. They deprive children of the opportunities to demonstrate what they are able to do. She argues that the purpose of school tasks is rarely made clear to young children. The Socratic questioning style of interaction of much classroom talk between the teacher and pupils forces children into an uneasy sense of always having to search for answers they believe the teacher wants to hear. Lastly, the kind of tasks offered to young children are often remote from their own experiences of learning in real-life situations. She challenges the belief that teachers should wait until children are 'ready' to move from concrete to abstract levels of thinking. Instead teachers should actively encourage children to move towards the 'disembedded thinking' which characterizes the 'formal' modes of learning in schools. Children should be encouraged to use talk to move from the here and now, freeing language from its embeddedness in present events. Teachers should model uses of language as a symbol system which empowers children with the ability to express their abstract thinking, *but* within learning contexts which are meaningful to the children.

> the normal child comes to school with well-established skills as a thinker. But his thinking is directed outwards on to the real, meaningful, shifting, distracting world. What is going to be required for success in our educational system is that he should learn to turn language and thought in upon themselves. He must be able to direct his own thought processes in a thoughtful manner. He must become able not just to talk but to choose what he will say, not just to interpret but to weigh possible interpretations. His conceptual system must expand in the direction of increasing ability to represent itself. He must become capable of manipulating symbols.
>
> (Donaldson 1978: 88–9)

In other words children should be *taught* how to extend their powers of thinking towards abstraction; we should not simply wait for it to happen.

A child must be 'ready' to move on to the next developmental stage and must not be forced to move on to a higher level of cognitive functioning

The cognitive curriculum

In the past teachers of young children have not emphasized cognitive develop-ment as high amongst their educational aims. In two studies of the aims of nursery teachers (Taylor *et al.* 1972; Clift *et al.* 1980) teachers overwhelmingly emphasized 'social' aims. This contrasts with traditions of early years education in the USA where cognitive development is emphasized at the levels of curriculum planning, regular testing and economic accountability. Because of the traditions of the English nursery school discussed in Chapter 1, there is still a strong resistance in our school cultures to what the Americans define as the Cognitive Curriculum (see e.g. Copple *et al.* 1979) and more recently the Highscope curriculum (Hohmann 1979). This in part explains the heated arguments raging over the efficacy of translating the Highscope system into British schools. The Highscope curriculum emphasizes the need for each child to be directly involved in planning his or her own activities, negotiated with an adult, by a method known as 'Plan-Do-Review'. Children are encouraged to set goals for themselves for the day's activities in the nursery and to reflect on how far they achieved these goals at the end of the session. For teachers imbued with the English nursery school tradition of free play, the Highscope curriculum is seen as too adult structured.

However, for many teachers of young children the new emphasis on teaching children how to think is exciting. The work of Vygotsky (1978) (for many years accessible only to Russian-speaking students but now available in English translation) emphasizes the role of internalized inner speech in structuring children's cognitive activities. This is a very different view of the role of language in learning from the Piagetian view. Piaget believed that language is the externalized evidence of children's active learning experiences rather than a tool for thinking. But Vygotsky also has a quite different view of the role of the adult in children's learning. He sees the process of human mental development as functioning at two levels – the actual, present level and the potential next level. He calls the gap between the two levels 'the zone of proximal development', and he sees the role of the teacher as directed towards encouraging children to move from the actual to the potential level of development. The teacher is to encourage children to do *without* help what they can do only at present *with* help. This process of teacher support for children's learning is what Bruner calls 'scaffolding' learning and will be referred to again in Chapter 3, which will focus on teachers' strategies. So there is a clear contrast between Vygotsky's view of the role of the teacher in actively working to improve children's levels of development and his view of know-ledge as acquired by essentially social and external processes, and Piaget's view of the teacher expertly setting up experiences by which the child will learn through his or her own individual actions and exploratory behaviours.

Schemas

There is interest too in the ways in which young children organize their learning experiences. For example Chris Athey (1981), working at the Froebel Institute, has been researching into schemas, which she defines as 'patterns of repeatable and generalisable actions which can be applied to objects or events'. Children in the nursery attached to the Institute were observed by staff and researchers, but parents were also encouraged to observe the children at home. Thus, the children were observed using schemas across a range of nursery and home-based activities.

One such schema is the topological space notion of 'enclosure' (see also Piaget and Inhelder 1956). It is characterized by an absorption with envel-oping space – e.g. the building of brick enclosures which are then used to represent a variety of imaginary objects such as a car, a boat, a castle. The schemas will then be explored in a whole variety of subsequent related exploratory activities. Athey gives the following example:

Over several months Louise systematically explored enveloping space and certain associated schemas. She always carefully wrapped things up. For instance, she wrapped her clay pancake up (it was too hot to hold). She went round covering things up. When she had covered up the windows of her model house she said, 'Now it's dark inside'. She covered a worm with sand saying: 'YOU know they live under the sand . . . at night he'll be asleep.' She made a hole right through her 'home' book. Her mother was embarrassed and carefully mended the book. Louise made 'a sofa with a hole in it'. She wrapped 'sausages' in tin foil to 'cook' them. She wrapped up her mother's shoes at home and 'posted the parcel' in the rubbish bin, 'the post box'. When she arrived in school she painted 'a parcel with mummy's shoes in it'. Using different materials, Louise told a long story (on audio tape) about her cat. The persistent theme was the cat going inside and outside the dustbin and bringing what was inside the dustbin into the house and so on. Her persistent concerns had become sufficiently internalised for her to have an interesting conversation about them.

(Athey 1980: 8)

Beryl McDougall, for many years an influential Early Years Adviser for Cleveland, pursued the study of schemas with nursery staff and parents in Cleveland Schools. In an edition of their newsletter, *Rumpus* (Nicholls 1986), McDougall gives another example of a child experimenting with a schema:

the action and muscular sensation of going round an object can be represented:
by language, i.e. the words 'going round' are symbols of the actual event
by another action, e.g. pushing a toy vehicle round the object
by graphics, e.g. drawing a circle.
Added complexity is again acquired when these representational schemas are coordinated as, for example, when the circle and the dab (in painting) are co-ordinated to create a face with eyes and nostrils or a body with buttons down the front.

(Athey in Nicholls, 1986: 6)

Once parents and teachers/nursery nurses are alerted to these recurring patterns of behaviour, they are less inclined to dismiss children's play behaviour as 'flitting'. They begin to make connections for the children between one set of play experiences and others. It may be that the child moves physically from running round and round a climbing frame, or later chants a continuous refrain about going 'round and round the garden like a teddy bear' as she plays with making circles with her fingers in the sand pit. Minutes later she might be pushing a toy fire engine round a pile of Lego. Her drawings and paintings over a period of weeks may show endless variations on large and small circle motifs.

Her behaviour in play is in fact the projection of different manifestations of a consistent preoccupation. She is trying to come to terms with roundness.

In the same *Rumpus* newsletter Chris Athey is quoted as saying:

> I was watching a child who was spinning his pencil on a table with a twist of his finger. I said, 'You're making it go round, aren't you?' Immediately he looked at me with interest. I mentioned some of the things I had seen going round, such as wheels and a cement mixer, and used the word 'rotate'. Excitedly he added things he knew. Once you show in your conversation with a child that you've cottoned on to his current schema, you're his friend for life.

> (Athey, in Nicholls, 1986: 21)

The schemas appear to serve the purpose for the young child of categorizing experiences or insights in order to make sense of them and are operating in a much more complex way than simply assigning verbal labels to like or unlike objects or events. As Jerome Bruner pointed out, there are tools of the mind as well as tools of the hand, and Athey's final comment is significant because it demonstrates an adult interest in sharing with a child the tools of thinking which are helping him to understand the world. It is true that what a child brings to a learning experience from his or her own previous learning is always novel, but equally true that the kind of *strategies* which learners are likely to use are identifiable and generalizable to any number of children. In other words, there is a difference between emphasizing the individuality of each child's past learning experiences and insisting that every child learns differently. Coming to an understanding of this may help the teachers of young children to see the task of educating a class of twenty-five 'individuals' as a more manageable prospect.

Metacognition

There is also new interest in children's understanding of their own thought processes, their awareness of how to cope with particular kinds of problems, their ability to remember – what is called 'metacognition'. Sara Meadows (Meadows and Cashdan 1988) points out that if children are helped to gain insights into how they think, plan, remember and set about different types of problems they are likely to gain confidence in tackling new tasks.

> Children are very commonly novices on tasks where adults have become experts with many well-learned routines. It is part of the process of education to facilitate the child's sharing of this expertise. It is important to recognise that it is both specific expertise – how to paint a straight line on the paper – and generalised expertise – how to hold tools, adjust their use to the particular task, judge where to start and where to stop, and so forth. A general 'feel' for the task as a whole is crucial.

> (Meadows and Cashdan 1988: 55–6)

Meadows believes that adults should provide role models for children by demonstrating their own planning, strategies for remembering things, or systematic approaches to solving problems. This is not to suggest that children should be drilled in 'strategies for thinking' in isolation from a real and perceived purpose. It is not appropriate for young children to be given lessons in problem-solving of the de Bono 'How to weigh an elephant' variety. In the home an apprenticeship model of learning is provided for children quite naturally. A parent might use a board in the kitchen where important notes about forthcoming school and family events are pinned up, shopping lists may be made before the weekly trip to the supermarket, or a sketch of where new floor covering is to be laid may be scribbled on the back of an envelope. This sharing of strategies for regulating behaviour and perhaps for saving time and minimizing frustration in achieving a goal is rarely in evidence in infant classrooms. Yet 'Thinking about your thinking seems to be an effective way of getting better at it, and also to be a source of self-confidence' (Meadows and Cashdan 1988: 56). There is no reason why young children should not also benefit from being given actual examples of how to think deliberately through problems as part of a negotiated system for organizing the day's learning activities. The Highscope model offers an example of how this can be achieved with individual children, but young children can also see the point of talking through with their teachers whole-class patterns of planning and the mechanics of functioning as a group in classrooms, and can benefit from working together on real problems such as access to cloakroom storage systems or maximizing the use of hall times.

Children learn through first-hand experiences, particularly through play activities

The value of play

Early years educators have always set a high value on children's ability to learn through play. In part this is a reflection of the importance they ascribe to learning through 'first-hand experiences'. A belief in the value of play has permeated through the kinds of ideologies reviewed in the first chapter. Play is seen to be an essential component of children's 'normal' development. This culturally based conviction is best crystallized in Susan Isaac's often quoted statement:

> Play is indeed the child's work, and the means whereby he grows and develops. Active play can be looked upon as a sign of mental health; and its absence, either of some inborn defect, or of mental illness.
>
> (Isaacs 1929)

In fact, as P. K. Smith and Cowie (1988: Ch. 5) point out in *Understanding Children's Development*, we have little empirical evidence upon which to base our belief in the value of play in young children's learning. After reviewing research studies which have been carried out, the authors conclude:

> Considerable empirical investigation has now been made into the benefits of play, but 'the jury is still out'. Most of the investigations have concentrated on the supposed cognitive benefits of play, and have been made in an explicitly educational framework. Yet, as we have seen, the evidence for strong cognitive benefits, either from theory, observation, correlational or experimental studies is not convincing. If anything, the evidence is better for the benefits of play for social competence. This has been less thoroughly studied; while the postulated benefits of play for emotional release and catharsis have scarcely received any well-controlled experimental study at all.
>
> (P. R. Smith and Cowie 1988: 139)

We have discussed Dearden's (1968) reference to the 'eulogizing of play', and there is a sense in which educators of young children have been accused of sentimentalizing play, reducing it to the level of idealization of those Mabel Lucie Atwell postcards of darling children at play, pretty, spotlessly clean, smiling and unreal. However, there may be another underlying and fundamental reason for the accusation that teachers of young children indulge in 'preciousness'. The fact is that 'play' has been defined as trivial by a male-dominated society which emphasizes the rational, scientific side of learning and the power of rational thought. Work is the serious, rational business of life and play is for leisure and fun.

Moreover, the concept of learning through play involves acknowledging the role of imagination and, dare one say it, the emotions in intellectual development. There is a profound distrust of any alternative imaginative/affective approach to education amongst the dominant scientific/rational tradition in education and, as was argued in Chapter 1, teachers of young children are inevitably caught up in the determining societal and political beliefs about the purpose and value of education. The elementary school tradition certainly put play in its 'proper' place – the self-contained and special times of Friday afternoons and 'playtime' in the yard, the territory of the children, well away from the boundaries of the serious business in classrooms. There are many infant schools where these patterns of 'play' are still operating; though the rhetoric of the profession would not lead one to expect to see such patterns in the 1990s.

What is play?

Dearden also points out that we have not clearly defined the characteristics of play. It is another of those words that tends to be used at a slogan-like level by teachers of young children. In infant schools play can be

1 rushing around the school playground

2 manipulating table-top toys
3 impersonating mums and dads in the house corner
4 joining in adult-directed and rule-bound games of lotto or Happy Families
5 simply 'horsing about'.

Attempts *have* been made to define types of play behaviour. For example Piaget distinguished between practice play, which involves repetition of actions until they are progressively mastered, symbolic play, which involves the manipulation of symbols, and games with rules (Piaget 1962). He argued that children will develop the ability to handle increasing levels of abstraction in their play behaviours – children aged 18 months may use a real brush to pretend to brush their hair, 3–4-year-olds might use a substitute body part such as their fingers to represent the brush, and 6–8-year-olds will probably simply use an imaginary brush to carry out the action.

A more sophisticated attempt to categorize play behaviours, but not by isolating them from other behaviours in a classroom, has been made by Meadows and Cashdan (1983) in a study of nursery classrooms. Play was rated, along with other behaviours, on dimensions such as social participation, degree of child's involvement, number of operations, themes or skills involved, extent to which materials were used and apparent goals of the child.

Purposes of play

It may be helpful to reflect briefly upon theoretical claims about the purposes of play. Theories about the function of play range from Karl Groos's view that play is preparation for life, or Stanley Hall's belief that play behaviours are a reflection of our evolutionary past, to the Freudian view that play provides a safe opportunity for children to come to terms with their wishes and anxieties. (For a full account of theories of play see the standard texts by Millar 1968 and Garvey 1977.)

If infant teachers are asked to address the issue of the function of play in children's development they are likely to suggest that play is important for physical development, for social development and the child's mental health, and for cognitive development; in all these aspects there are clear references back to 'classic' theories of the function of play. Each of these three functions will be discussed.

1. Play promoting physical development

If we take the function of play as promoting the physical development of the child, there is evidently a spontaneous urge amongst young children to try out and practise physical activities for the sake of enjoyment and the sense of achievement they gain from progressive mastery of large motor skills such as running, jumping, climbing, kicking and catching balls, etc. Fine motor skills are practised in activities such as building blocks, posting shapes into containers and mark making. These skills are clearly transferred to the real tasks of, for

example, moving around to gain independence, or manipulating clothes in the
tricky business of getting dressed without adult help. We tend to forget how
rapidly young children are developing a whole range of physical accomplish-
ments in their first years at school and how much their self esteem is bound up
with progressive mastery of physical skills. Montessori's curriculum provided
carefully structured opportunities for the mastery of physical skills; it is
interesting to note that Piaget carried out his early research into children's
learning at a modified Montessori school and was for many years president of
the Swiss Montessori Society. Piaget saw the functions of play as consolidating
existing skills by practising known schemas with minor variations and also as
giving the child a sense of 'ego continuity' as they gained confidence through
the mastery of physical actions in a climate where it was safe to fail. Expressing
this concept of mastery in another way, Bruner wrote, 'Play provides an
excellent opportunity to try combinations of behaviour that wouldn't be tried
under functional pressure' (Bruner 1972).

2. Play promoting social development and the child's mental health

The function of play in promoting social development is often taken for
granted but as we have already indicated has not been well researched, and is
rarely systematically provided for in schools. Social development will be
discussed on pp. 38–41.

The related concept of play as a therapeutic process, an agent of mental
hygiene, is a legacy, through Susan Isaacs' work (Isaacs 1948) and Melanie
Klein's influence (Klein 1949) of the Freudian tradition. There is new evidence
that we have underestimated children's competencies in learning to handle the
emotional demands of relationships. For example, Judy Dunn's research
(reported in Bruner and Haste 1987: ch. 1) indicates that far from being so
egocentric that they were unable to empathize with another's point of view,
2-year-olds were able to demonstrate their awareness of and understanding of
the feelings of other members of the family. They demonstrated this understanding in talk and behaviour towards others. In the following example, talk
was stimulated by a 2-year-old, Virginia L., looking at a book with her mother.

Child: Great big bonfire.
Mother: Big bonfire, yes, it is a great big bonfire. What is it burning up the
           bonfire?
Child: Burning birdies. All hungry.
Mother: They've got to fly away because they've burned the tree that the birdies
           used to live in, haven't they? And look at all the little bunny rabbits
           crying.
Child: They sad.
Mother: That's right, they're sad.

(Bruner and Haste 1987: 33)

The children in Dunn's study also demonstrated that they understood how to be agents of pleasure, comfort or pain by their actions which included affectionate physical responses, comforting siblings or parents in obvious distress and deliberate teasing. She describes one very sophisticated teasing strategy used by a 2-year-old. Her older sister had three pretend friends named Lily, Allelluia and Peepee. If the sisters argued, the 2-year-old would announce that *she* was Allelluia and revel in her older sister's obvious sense of outrage! Many examples of playing out feeling states were observed in the children's pretend play. It was also apparent that children whose parents spoke to them about feelings were more likely to articulate their own ideas about emotional states. Significantly the research indicated that mothers talked more often about feelings to girl children, who in turn produced more talk about feelings than boys. These findings are important when set alongside recent evidence about differences between women and men in the way they refer to feelings in talking about moral issues and have important implications for the education of boys and girls at all levels of schooling (Gilligan 1982).

We have already referred to the tendency for the education of the emotions to be regarded with grave suspicion within our male dominated 'stiff upper lip' culture. Infant teachers are aware of the power of children's emotional reactions to events both in school and in their lives outside, but perhaps because of pressures to concentrate on the tried and tested basic skills curriculum, they are not acknowledging the importance of structuring oppor-tunities in their curriculum planning for children to come to terms with both the positive and negative effects of feelings or the skills of developing relationships with others. The arts are an obvious area in which children can be encouraged to explore feelings within a safe framework (this theme will be returned to in Chapter 5 on the curriculum in infant schools) but there is a great deal of scope in many collaborative learning activities for social development and the expression of feelings to be much more overtly 'taught'.

One particularly fascinating line of research has been into what Csiksent-mihalyi (1979) calls 'flow' in play events. The Froebelian view of play as being a highly spiritual activity for the child, mediating between the emotions, spirit and intellect, the unfolding of the divine 'essence' of the child, is extended through Csiksentmihalyi's work. 'Flow' is characterized by that blissful sense of involvement that adults can recapture in pursuits such as listening to music, rock-climbing, dancing, sexual activities or indeed in some cases academic work! The involvement is total – a loss of self-consciousness, but at the same time an awareness of being in control of the self's absorption in the activity. In this instance it might be children who can teach adults a thing or two. The ease with which they can become totally absorbed in an activity and sustain that absorption over long periods of time can be impressive. It demonstrates that children, given the appropriate learning conditions, *can* concentrate for long periods.

3. *Play promoting intellectual development*

The third function that teachers claim for play in infant classrooms is that of promoting intellectual development. Evidence is thin on the ground to support this claim, and in fact what evidence we have makes depressing reading. It is in pre-school settings that most research has been done into levels of cognitive challenge in play. Meadows and Cashdan (1983) found that the free play offered to the children in twenty nursery school classes in an Outer London borough did not appear to challenge them intellectually:

> Life was pleasant enough for most of the children – fights, quarrels or upsets were rare – but so were discovery, achievement after endeavour and intellectual challenge. Some play bouts were brief and desultory, some went on interminably at the same repetitive activity, as if the child couldn't get out of a rut. Some of the rising fives were clearly bored with the available curriculum and were getting their kicks out of rough and tumble or other social activities. Some children managed a choice of activities that took them out of the teacher's orbit completely, apart from token compliance with story sessions. Others, less boisterous, remained on the margins of activities, drifting unengaged from one space to another without even sustaining either conversation or involvement with task or material. Though the classroom norm was happy, goal-directed use of the resources provided, enough children fell below this level, and so few rose to the heights of creativity, cooperation and challenge, that we could not feel the free play curriculum was fulfilling our hopes.
>
> (Meadows and Cashdan 1983: 35)

In another major study, again of pre-school provision, in this case using playgroups and nursery classes and schools in Oxfordshire to collect evidence, Kathy Sylva and her colleagues (Sylva *et al*. 1980) observed the learning behaviour of children. They made an analysis of the level of cognitive challenge offered by play activities within the nursery curriculum. High yield of cognitive challenge – defined by the challenge of the task and the way in which the child carried it out – was achieved when children were involved in music (when not led by an adult), small-scale construction, art (where children choose their own medium), large-scale construction and structured materials. The qualities which were common to these activities were that they had clear goals and involved materials that provided 'real world feedback'; that is 'They show the child whether a given sequence of behaviours has "worked" or hasn't' (Sylva *et al*. 1980: 63). Moderate yield of cognitive challenge was achieved in pretend, scale version or manipulation activities; and low yield in non-playful interaction, informal games and rule-bound games, and gross motor play. However, in these 'moderate and low yield' activities, there was often a high degree of social interaction between the children. The final group of activities, 'the lowest yield', including social play, horsing around and giggling, 'seemed motivated by the desire for the pleasure of physical exercise or of repetition'. They offered the children little opportunity for planning or elaborating play behaviours.

Sylva's team also investigated the length of time children concentrated on play activities – and at this level of analysis, pretend play scored highly along with the activities already defined as offering a high level of cognitive challenge. Finally, the team observed that children achieved levels of complex play with a high degree of cognitive challenge when they were playing in pairs or in social groups paralleled to others, and in the case of the 4-year-olds (rather than the 3-year-olds) observed, when in the company of an adult.

It is difficult to find hard evidence from infant classrooms about the level of intellectual challenge of play experiences in which children engage. In a study of infant classrooms in the now defunct ILEA (Tizard *et al.* 1988) there was little evidence of *any* kinds of play activities in the classes of 7-year-olds studied. In a recent study of 4-year-olds in infant classrooms (N. Bennett and Kell 1989) fewer than 6 per cent of all activities observed were categorized as 'play' and 'play was used as a filler activity of unclear purposes'. (Both these studies will be discussed in detail in Chapter 4 when we examine the curriculum offered in infant classrooms.)

Children need to develop competence in language use to function effectively as school learners

Many infant teachers working in classrooms in the 1990s were trained within the traditions of the 'deficit model' of language development. Through the work of Basil Bernstein (1971, 1975) and Joan Tough (1976) in particular, we were encouraged to focus on children's levels of language competence which were identified by their use of increasingly complex language structures, and their ability to use language for a greater variety of purposes. The role of the adult was seen to be one of fostering the child's progress towards greater levels of competence by styles of questioning, or by demonstrating different ways of using language. Working-class children were seen to need this kind of adult support far more than middle-class children.

The role of discourse

Recent thinking about the role of language in children's cognitive development has switched the emphasis to the role of discourse in children's language development. The shift parallels the emphasis on the child learning as a social being rather than as an individual explorer of the world. There is also a much greater concentration on what children *can* do with language rather than what they cannot do. Language development is seen as a social process, and in order to study children's linguistic capabilities research studies have adopted methodologies which allow the child to be studied in the social context which is most natural to them – that is at home rather than exclusively in school or in a laboratory.

This has had unfortunate consequences in one sense. Teachers are being told that the styles of interaction they adopt in schools disadvantage children in that they offer a restricted number of daily adult–child interactions in comparison to those offered at home and that the quality of school adult–child interactions is inferior to that offered in homes regardless of the class label given to that home. One of the most influential studies of this kind has been Tizard and Hughes' study of the language use of a sample of 4-year-old girls, fifteen of whom were defined as working class and fifteen as middle class, both at home and in their nursery classes (Tizard and Hughes 1984). The study demonstrated that working-class girls in particular were given little opportunity to engage in sustained adult–child discourse in nursery classes. The girls received more frequent sustained and challenging opportunities for talk in their own homes. Although the patterns of adult–child talk at home can illuminate teachers' understandings of the cognitive and social benefits of one-to-one dialogues, my view is that it is unreasonable to expect teachers to operate in this way in nursery and infant classrooms. Schools are simply not able to be like homes. Teachers are managing not one or two but many young children during their day. However, that is *not* to argue that teachers should not try to improve the quality of their discourse with pupils.

A much more extensive study of children's language development has been based at Bristol University as part of a fifteen year longitudinal research study (Wells 1987). Gordon Wells emphasizes the reciprocal roles of adults and children when they are talking to each other. Children do not simply imitate the language of those around them, but as Naom Chomsky (1976) argued, they are actively involved in generating their own versions of speech. Nevertheless the language of the community around them shapes the conventions of both language production and language use that the child will adopt. Wells points out that most adults intuitively moderate their language to the level at which the child can respond – when parents do so we call this 'motherese' – by for example shortening their utterances, emphasizing particular words, repeating and paraphrasing what the child has said. He likens these instinctive adjustments to the linguistic capabilities of a child to the strategies an adult will adopt when teaching a child how to catch a ball. Wells also emphasizes, as Margaret Donaldson does, the importance of language use being embedded in contexts in which the adult and the child have shared experiences in common from which to draw shared meanings:

> What seems to be more important [than quantity] is that, to be most helpful, the child's experience of conversation should be in a one to one situation in which the adult is talking about matters that are of interest and concern to the child, such as what he or she is doing, has done or plans to do, or about activities in which the child and adult engage

together. The reason for this is the fact that, when both child and adult are engaged in a shared activity, the chances are maximised that they will be attending to the same objects and events and interpreting the situation in similar ways.

(Wells 1987: 44)

Storying

Wells also examines the role of 'storying' in developing children's thinking. 'Constructing stories in the mind – or storying as it has been called – is one of the most fundamental means of making meaning; as such it is an activity that pervades all aspects of learning' (Wells 1987: 194). There has been a growing interest in the power of metaphor and the narrative mode to encapsulate abstract ideas and make them accessible to children and adults. Rosen wrote, 'Every chemical reaction is a story compressed into the straitjacket of an equation. Every car speeds down the road by virtue of the well-known engineer's yarn called the Otto cycle' (Rosen 1984). For children the function of narrative can be to enable them to move from the here and now of their immediate experiences, to the more distanced ideas about what happened then and what might happen next. In other words the narrative form is a potent resource to help children to move to abstractions.

Stories have the additional advantage of engaging the emotions. It has already been suggested that emotional engagement is an aspect of learning which has been underrated and under-researched in early years education. Infant teachers know instinctively that children learn and remember things best when they are having fun, gaining emotional as well as intellectual satisfaction from an activity, and most stories are enjoyable shared experiences in classrooms. What is novel is the idea that stories may also serve the function of empowering children to think in more abstract ways.

The oral tradition

There is a further interesting development in the power of language to help children's thinking which parallels research into the way in which oral cultures are maintained. For example the long and complex songs of Aborigines, which are passed down from generation to generation, appear to be remembered by units of sound rather than words. In oral cultures, crucial patterns of beliefs are fixed in the minds of the participating communities by the repetition of rhymes, rhythms etc.

Education in such cultures is largely a matter of constantly immersing the young into the enchanting patterns of sound until they resound to the patterns, until they become 'artistically' in tune with, harmonious with, the institutions of their culture.

(Egan 1988: 98)

Perhaps shared nursery rhymes, finger rhymes, traditional tales, skipping and tagging chants, and traditional songs provide for the young child a sense of security in a shared past – something that is common to grandparents, parents, teachers, siblings, cousins – and we should be working more consciously within schools to nurture what is left of British oral traditions and to introduce all children to the exciting additional oral traditions being introduced into the United Kingdom by, for example, Asian and Afro-Caribbean cultures.

In social development children move from egocentrism to the ability to empathize with others

Social development and schooling

It has already been pointed out that teachers of young children rank social development as high amongst the aims they identify for early years education, and yet in general they are not clear about how these complex processes of learning to be 'sociable' in a range of contexts work. However there is some interesting research evidence into the way in which children learn to understand and operate social conventions. Far more emphasis is being placed on the significance of the social contexts and mores within which a child develops as we are beginning to understand that the child is held within the culture of the family, community, school and society – nesting one inside each other like the casings of a Russian doll.

When children enter school they are faced with a new set of social conventions and relationships for which even the experience of a playgroup or nursery school may not have prepared them (see Cleave *et al.* 1982). The intimacy of a small family setting will certainly not have done so. The strategies the teacher adopts to socialize school entrants into appropriate behaviours will be discussed in Chapter 3.

There is evidence that children use 'scripts' (Nelson 1977) to understand routine events in their lives in the same way that adults do. Both adults and children can find the strangeness of entering into a novel set of routines fairly stressful. Think about the last time you moved house, or changed jobs. It is the very fact that you cannot predict what will happen next that is so unnerving. What time are the tea and coffee breaks? When will the gas board official come to read the meter? Where can I park my car, or buy a stamp, or find a milkman? What do my workmates/neighbours expect of me? There is plenty of evidence that coming to terms with the strange rituals of classrooms is stressful for children starting school. Nelson claims that children quickly establish for themselves an idea of the likely sequence of events that make up a school day. Within this mental map, they are then free to concentrate on unfamiliar or unexpected events and the significance of these for that particular moment. However, it is clear that for many immature and anxious children, any departure from what they come to see as the normal classroom routine can

throw them into a state of distress – hence the tears over hall times or the arrival
of a supply teacher.   •

Learning to be a social being

Apart from trying to come to terms with the conventions of an institution
geared to the needs of many, rather than a family life geared to the needs of a
small group, the child also has to learn how to be a social being. The
conventions of making friends may be unknown to a child. One important set
of skills is strategies for entry to a group. Rubin (1980), in his book *Children's
Friendships*, describes this account by Corsaro of a 4-year-old gaining access to
a group in a nursery school:

> Two girls, Jenny and Betty, are playing around a sandbox in the outside
> courtyard of the school. I am sitting on the ground near the sandbox
> watching. The girls are putting sand in pots, cupcake pans, bottles and
> teapots. . . . Another girl, Debbie, approaches and stands near me observ-
> ing the other two girls. Neither Jenny nor Betty acknowledges her
> presence. Debbie does not speak to me or the other girls, and no one
> speaks to her. After watching for some time (five minutes or so) she
> circles the sandbox three times and stops again and stands near me. After
> a few more minutes of watching, Debbie moves to the sandbox and
> reaches for a teapot in the sand. Jenny takes the pot away from Debbie
> and mumbles, 'No'. Debbie backs away and again stands near me
> observing the activity of Jenny and Betty. Then she walks over next to
> Betty, who is filling the cupcake pan with sand. Debbie watches Betty for
> just a few seconds, then says:
> 'We're friends, right? We're friends, right, Betty?'
> Betty, not looking up at Debbie and while continuing to place sand in the
> pan, says, 'Right'.
> 'I'm making coffee,' Debbie says to Betty.
> 'I'm making cupcakes,' Betty replies.
> Betty turns to Jenny and says, 'We're mothers, right, Jenny?'
> Jenny replies, 'Right.'
> The three 'mothers' continue to play together for twenty more minutes,
> until the teacher announces clean-up time.
>
> (Corsaro 1979: 320–1)

Using careful observations of this kind Corsaro built up a picture of the way in
which children learned to gain access to activities and to establish friendships.
Children had to learn to overcome initial rejections, here illustrated in
Corsaro's fieldnotes by Debbie's refusal to submit to Jenny's rejecting strategies designed to exclude her from the group around the sandbox. Children
also had to learn how to *be* a friend. They had to learn how to give and take in
sharing toys and attention. They had to learn how to manage conflict, not only

how to express their own feelings but also how to empathize with the feelings of others. In many cases they learned by trial and error and by observing what worked and what did not work in making and keeping friends amongst the models offered by their peer group, but it appears to help if adults encourage children to reflect consciously on what they have learned. The role of the adult in supporting social development is to demonstrate conventions, to explain the processes involved and give feedback of both a positive and negative kind in encouraging children to develop the skills of making and keeping friends.

Gender issues in social development

There is evidence from classroom-based research (Mullin *et al.* 1987; Clarricoates 1980; Spender 1982; Weiner 1985) that the social conventions of gender-appropriate behaviour are reinforced by interactions between both peer group and adult–child in schools. Boys and girls tend to gravitate to single-sex groupings even at pre-school level. On the whole boys opt for boisterous, large motor play, operate more confidently in all aspects of outdoor physical play, and choose areas to play where adult (usually female) attention is not often directed (e.g. in the construction play or outdoor sandpit areas). Girls opt for more 'domestic' activities such as house play and for table-top toys where adults are more likely to be near at hand. Both genders devise strategies to exclude each other from same sex groupings. Browne and France (1986) describe the adult talk and behaviour towards boys and girls which reinforces sexist stereotypes in 'Only cissies wear dresses: a look at sexist talk in the nursery', but the issue of teacher strategies in relating to children from different race, class and gender will be addressed in more detail in Chapter 4.

The development of morality

Finally, interest is beginning to be shown in the way in which young children learn about morality. Until recently research into the development of moral reasoning was based on refinements of Piaget's study (Piaget 1932). Piaget pioneered the method of eliciting children's responses to stories which presented some moral dilemma. He asked the children what they believed was the right thing to do in such a situation. Children's ideas about lying, destroying property, etc. and about punishments and fairness were taken from the discussions about the stories. Piaget also used games of marbles to elicit children's beliefs about rules. He demonstrated that children move from a morality of constraint, where strict and unchangeable rules derived from adult authority were imposed on them from outside, to a morality of autonomy, where there was no longer a blind obedience to outside authority, where punishments were considered to be for righting wrongs rather than expiation, where rules may be modified by democratic processes within a group and where justice must take account of extenuating circumstances.

Building on Piaget's work, Kohlberg (1976) also used the method of presenting children with moral dilemmas couched in stories. He identified six stages of moral development, but overall he believed that children moved from a *Pre-Conventional level*, characterized by a concern for personal interests, the avoidance of punishments, and obedience to authority based on fear rather than respect; to a *Conventional level*, where laws and duties are seen as necessary to maintain stability in society and where it is winning approval from one's immediate social group that is important (most adolescents and adults stay at this level); to a *Post-Conventional level* where laws are respected because of a belief in universal moral principles such as liberty, equal rights and the dignity of human life.

The methodology used by Piaget and Kohlberg has been criticized for providing children with adult views of moral dilemmas and, as in Donaldson's critique of Piaget's work on the development of scientific and mathematical thinking, for constraining children's opportunities to demonstrate what they know and understand in their own terms and contexts. Feminist critiques have also argued that the hierarchy of stages of morality presented by male researchers rank justice above compassion and love (see Gilligan 1982) and argue that from a female perspective it is not enough to *understand* what is right and wrong. One must also *care*.

Turiel (1978) has explored children's understanding of morality and social conventions and demonstrated that even young children can differentiate between important moral rules such as not hurting people and less important social rules such as whether one should wear clothes to come to school or practical rules such as cleaning one's teeth. Haste (1987) describes the processes by which children learn to decode 'the grammar of social relationships' by interacting with others as individuals but within the culturally defined norms of groups. Primary teachers rate social learning and the gaining of a sense of morality high amongst their aims for primary education: Ashton *et al.* (1975) found that teachers ranked third 'The child should be beginning to acquire a set of moral values on which to base his own behaviour, e.g. honesty, sincerity, personal responsibility'. Despite this there is very little school-based research, teaching materials or guidelines for infant schools to support teachers of young children in putting these aims into practice.

Every child is an individual learning in his or her own unique way

The Plowden statement, 'At the heart of the education process lies the child', and the catch-phrase 'child-centred education' are often used by teachers of young children to defend their decisions about teaching strategies, approaches to classroom organization and curriculum planning. In the late 1980s these tenets were used rather desperately to argue against the imposition of a subject-based National Curriculum upon young children.

Although every child (and indeed every adult) does bring a unique set of experiences and understandings to each new learning situation and gradually constructs his or her own view of the world, it *is* possible, and as far as the teacher is concerned *essential*, to see that there are patterns in the development of learning across children's responses and behaviours. Unless teachers of young children acknowledge and articulate these generalizable patterns, they are faced with an insurmountable task in planning and implementing a curriculum which fosters learning in a class of up to thirty-five children. Of course, it is important to retain insights into the particularities of each child as a learner and to respect their individuality, but it is equally important to acknowledge their similarities.

Teachers learning about children's learning

For teachers of young children, time spent in close observation of their pupils engaged in learning should be a regular part of how they organize their teaching time. In most cases infant teachers have the advantage, because of the way they organize their classrooms and their teaching styles, of being able to work at close quarters with their pupils. Ideally they should become skilful at constructing their own theories about children's learning from the myriads of specific teaching and learning episodes to which they bear close witness every working day

An infant teacher who had trained herself to work in this way, using a range of techniques – including a video camera – to collect information about teaching and learning episodes, wrote:

> Children learn if they are given meaningful tasks where they can see a purpose in the activities. I know it is also important that they should be working in a fairly relaxed atmosphere so that they are not afraid to have a go at things, not afraid of making mistakes. But I've also recognised that there is a sense in which they take their cues from me – from my facial expression, my body language, the tone of my voice. So if I show that I have higher expectations of what they can do, then they will respond to those. I know also that they need to be able to access resources and equipment without having to keep asking me – they shouldn't have to have that kind of dependence on me. They need to be able to get on with each other. That also saves me a lot of time. But I've learned the hard way that that does not happen without us working at it. They have to learn how to work together. It doesn't just happen. Then they need lots of practical situations to try things out.

> (Anning 1987)

Another infant teacher who had observed children's learning in a similar way wrote:

I see the process of children's learning as:

(a) responding to an initial stimulus
(b) being given some idea by an adult of how to go about a task – for example some skills demonstrated or materials explained – to enable the children to do something
(c) being given a clear goal
(d) time to enable all the input to work in the child's own head so that maybe he can produce something related to the stimulus or theme which is uniquely his own.

She added:

The time could appear to be spent non-productively. For example a child going away to quietly work with Lego may be planning and thinking. Some teachers find this difficult to justify as learning time, but I don't.

(Anning 1987)

It is these 'common-sense' theories, developed through a critical reflexiveness towards what they already know, that provide teachers with the insights to address other people's theories, including psychological models, in a more confident and receptive way. There is, as we have seen, so much fascinating research into young children's learning now in progress. In reading about the research and at the same time closely observing children's learning behaviours in their own classrooms, teachers may address themselves to the gap between theory and practice identified on pp. 20–2.

For example to counter an argument either for or against a Behaviourist or Developmental model of children's learning with such clearly defined general principles as those articulated by the two infant teachers quoted above *must* be more effective than simply to repeat vague slogans about child-centredness. To understand how children learn to be social beings must help teachers to structure learning activities in the classroom or to respond sensitively to incidents in the playground so that they can guide children towards effective strategies for forming and sustaining friendships. This is the kind of professionalism that many primary teachers are now developing.

The process of developing this kind of professional knowledge can be represented in diagrammatic form as in Figure 2.

Teachers generate their theories through a continuous process of reflection in action. They plan on the basis of their past experiences of children learning. A specific classroom behaviour they encounter feeds back into and refines further their general understanding of children's learning behaviours. They modify their teaching strategies for their next set of plans. It is a cyclical process.

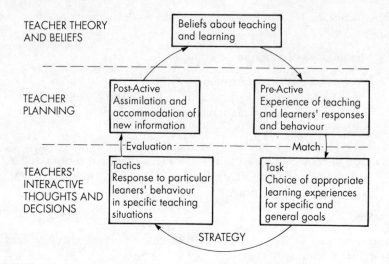

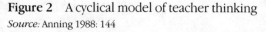

Figure 2   A cyclical model of teacher thinking
Source: Anning 1988: 144

It is towards the implementation of their professional knowledge into classroom teaching strategies, represented in the bottom sector of Figure 2, that we now turn.

3

Teachers teaching

The status of early years teachers

The kinds of strategies that teachers of young children use are the subject of a great deal of confusion and misunderstanding, amongst both practitioners and commentators on early years schooling. In the world at large they are often the source of the kind of amusement typified by the English actress, Joyce Grenfell's unforgettable sketches of a harassed infant teacher at work. She portrayed vividly the bizarre rituals of a teacher trying with stern but smiling fortitude to control a class of young children. But what is rarely acknowledged is the level of professional challenge that is inherent in the infant teacher's task. Teachers must ensure that classes of up to thirty-five children make progress in the conventional school learning of literacy, numeracy and knowledge about the world. At the same time they must induct them into the conventions of school culture.

Yet it is still not uncommon for secondary-trained teachers to be offered jobs teaching infant classes, presumably on the basis that anybody (particularly if they are female) can teach young children. An infant-trained teacher would rarely be offered work in the secondary sector, unless they were to work with children with special educational needs – in itself a dubious slur on that particular expertise at secondary level. It is also not uncommon for secondary-trained tutors in university, polytechnic and college education departments, whose teaching experience may in fact have been restricted to grammar schools only, to be training students to work with young children. The requirements of CATE have specified that tutors of students in initial training should have substantial, recent and relevant school experience of working in classrooms with the age range of children for whom they are training students.

However, most ex-secondary school tutors training students to work in primary schools elect to do their compulsory term of 'recent and relevant' experience every five years with junior age ranges, where understandably they feel more at ease. Moreover, the decimation of training college departments in the 1970s, many of which had impressive tutor expertise in the education of 3–8-year-olds, has had unfortunate long-term consequences for teacher supply. In 1971 there were 148 public sector institutions where teachers were trained; by 1984 these had been reduced to 54. Many of the courses closed were BEd routes into teaching, the traditional source of early years teachers in the UK. As a result, in the 1990s there is a worrying shortfall in the number of newly qualified teachers who are trained to work in nursery and infant classes.

It is a long haul to get the expertise of early years teachers recognized and given the status it deserves. But to some degree it must be acknowledged that early years practitioners themselves have been to blame. They have been reluctant to articulate their professional knowledge. Early Years Cliques have tended to feed on their own shared understandings. This was partly a defensive reaction to the low status in which they felt that their expertise was held by other educators. On the whole infant teachers were not encouraged to study for higher degrees, and so they lacked the skills or confidence to analyse the complex strategies they were using in classrooms. As a consequence, what little research has been done in infant classrooms has been by researchers with little 'inside' knowledge of teaching very young children.

In a sense even the quality of people who opt to become early years teachers is perhaps a self-selected type, through the combined processes of schools career counselling and the interviews for entry into initial training programmes. A 'type' of school pupil, student or young teacher who demonstrates strong views, who dresses slightly unorthodoxly or who is academically able would be unlikely to make it into the nursery or infant school system. For instance in King's (1978) study of infant school cultures, the headteachers whom he interviewed had definite views on the ideal infant teacher type:

> Her classroom was clean and tidy, although decked with the children's products. She completed her administrative tasks correctly: marking the register, collecting the dinner money, distributing notes for the children to take home. She came early in the morning and did not leave until school finished. She came in before term started. She gave a good performance in assembly. The quality of her craftwork was high. She showed professional pleasantness, affection and equanimity; she had a 'very good manner' and 'likes her children'.
>
> (King 1978: 73)

The 'typical infant teacher' is thus characterized as a conformist and compliant type. There is no reference to her (and she is universally seen to *be* female) intellectual ability or professional knowledge, other than in relation to the most mundane routine activities.

Once a young teacher enters early years education, he or she is quickly socialized into the cultural norms of certain well-established routines of teacher behaviours. In referring to Figure 1 (page 18) I argued that these routines are far more influential on young teachers' daily strategies in classrooms than the ideologies presented to them in programmes of initial training or in staffroom talk.

At the same time, because primary school teachers tend to be strongly imbued with a sense of their professional competence as inextricably bound up with their sense of self as competent people (see the seminal work of Jenny Nias 1989), their awareness of the gap between the ideologies they claim to espouse and the strategies they actually use creates enormous tensions and feelings of guilt. When 'outsiders' have identified the gaps between their theories and their practice, teachers have reacted with genuine pain. It *is* important to acknowledge the debilitating, emotional reactions of the teachers of young children to the kinds of negative criticisms they have received from research findings. Yet, in my experience, it is only when teachers face up to the gap between their 'espoused theories' and their 'theories in use' (Argyris and Schon 1976) that they begin to make sense of their habitual teaching strategies, recognize their strengths as well as their weaknesses and become realistic in their analysis of what is possible in infant classrooms.

The dilemma language

The 'dilemma' language, demonstrated in the absorbing account of the American husband and wife team, Ann and Harold Berlak (1981), who came to England to explore 'informal' primary education as it was practised, seems to be particularly useful to primary teachers as a tool for analysing their strategies in classrooms. Infant teachers face dilemmas created by conflicting roles in responding to the need both to instruct children and yet at the same time to control their behaviour in the classroom, and in reconciling the demands of external agencies – both parents and other professionals – with their own professional judgements about what is expected of them. These three areas of potential conflict – teacher as instructor, teacher as agent of control, and teacher as respondent to external pressures – and the effects on their teaching strategies, will be discussed in turn.

Teacher as instructor

To intervene or not to intervene?

One of the most obvious dilemmas for teachers is to reconcile their role as direct instructors with their role in indirectly nurturing the learning of young children. The conflict in roles can be traced directly back to the different traditions of schooling, the elementary and the progressive (delineated in Chapter 1) and the polarization between a Behaviourist and a developmental view of children's learning (identified in Chapter 2). On the one hand, teachers see their role as being responsible for teaching children the kind of knowledge that is deemed desirable by society and, on the other, they see their role as guiding children through a voyage of discovery towards their own personal knowledge.

Many infant teachers claim that they prefer to adopt a 'progressive' approach to education and espouse a non-interventionist stance towards promoting young children's learning. They prefer children to find things out for themselves, preferably through first-hand, practical, play activities. Their role is simply to structure the learning environment so that children can take advantage of the opportunities to learn that are provided within the school day. Yet at the same time they feel compelled to intervene in children's learning in a very direct way in the teaching of literacy and numeracy.

Observations of teachers working in infant classrooms have identified two clear consequences of this schizoid approach to teaching young children. It is clear that teachers tend to spend most of their time interacting with the children who are engaged in 'basic skills' activities. They appear to be responding partly to pressures from outside the school to concentrate on children's acquisition of literacy and numeracy. There is plenty of evidence that parents value these aspects of beginning schooling above all others – where the stated priorities of teachers are quite different.

In a recent study of 4-year-olds in schools in Rochdale, Wigan and Calderdale based at the Children's Centre at Leeds University (D. Bennett 1987) the infant teachers interviewed rated as high among their aims for educating the children: developing personal qualities such as self-confidence and independence, and positive attitudes to learning such as enjoyment, a sense of achievement, and satisfaction from learning. They also ranked the development of moral judgement, language and social skills as important. However, ninety-six parents of the 4-year-olds expected their children to learn reading, writing and arithmetic.

> Comments were made like 'letters, reading, counting, they're important' . . . 'practice things, maths, reading, writing' . . . 'do a few odd sums but not take aways' . . . Of the parents, only three made statements like 'I'm content if he's happy and wants to learn' . . . 'sure and confident' . . . 'able to develop at his own pace', three spoke of obedience and discipline and one of continuing nursery education. The majority of parents wanted their children to go to school, 'she's bright, I want her pushed a bit' . . . 'ready and eager to learn' . . . 'It's time . . . the first seven years are the time to learn'.
>
> (D. Bennett 1987: 21)

There are of course equally strong pressures from within the educational system on teachers to instruct children in the basics. Until a national system of testing was set up in 1988 through the Schools Examination and Assessment Council (SEAC), most primary schools formally tested children only in reading and numeracy. Some tests were imposed by local authority requirements – often at points of transfer – for example at 7 and 11 when children moved from infant to junior and from junior to secondary sectors. But teachers also know that their colleagues within schools make judgements about 'good' teachers on the progress of their pupils in 'the basics'. It is not surprising then that these are the aspects of school learning towards which teachers direct their attention. Nor is it surprising that they adopt didactic approaches to teaching the basics. They are, after all, repeating patterns they have learned at their own primary school teachers' knees! And those primary teachers in their turn were reflecting the persistent traditions and aspirations of the elementary school tradition.

Yet we have seen that infant teachers are also strongly influenced by the ideologies of progressive education. So the second major effect of the teacher intervention or non-intervention dilemma is that they adopt a decidedly *laissez-faire* approach towards teaching the rest of the infant curriculum – what Robin Alexander (1984) has called Curriculum II – the humanities, arts, physical and moral development. (Science and technology sit unhappily between the two approaches as pressure to teach these relatively new areas of the infant curriculum is imposed by the dictates of the National Curriculum – see Chapter 5.)

The non-interventionist stance towards teaching Curriculum II is expressed in the lack of overt teacher time given to interacting with children when they are engaged in topic work, or creative or practical play activities. These areas of the curriculum are often relegated to 'choosing time' and serve the function of keeping groups of children 'busy' while the teacher can get on with the 'real' work of teaching the basics. Teachers justify this disproportionate division of their time by claiming that children need the time and opportunity to express themselves creatively, to learn from playing with each other, and to learn from self-chosen, first-hand experiences. In this way they struggle to reconcile the conflicting imperatives of teacher-directed and child-centred approaches to teaching and learning.

The complexity of teaching strategies

The simplistic descriptions of primary teachers as formal or informal (N. Bennett 1976), or didactic or exploratory (DES 1978a), or into the four teacher types – individual monitors, class enquirers, group instructors and style changers – identified in the Oracle research (Galton *et al.* 1980) do not take into account the complexity of teacher thinking and action in classrooms.

How do infant teachers describe their own behaviours? It seems that they find it difficult to do so. When Jennifer Nias (1988) asked six primary teachers to define informal teaching they found the exercise impossible. They *were* able to describe formal teaching and to state that this was one of the repertoire of teaching strategies they used (sometimes more than they wished they did). So turning her original question on its head, Nias then asked the teachers to give an account of a teaching situation where they had *not* been teaching formally. In this way, by concentrating on specific episodes rather than general explanations, she was able to encourage teachers to describe informal teaching. They were then able to identify characteristics of the teaching/learning episodes described which were common to the accounts. Informal teaching occurred when children adopted a teacher's original teaching stimulus and made it their own; when the children were engaged in purposeful and personally meaningful activities; when they worked collaboratively; and when they used the teacher as a resource rather than an instructor.

It is possible, working in this teacher sympathetic way, to help teachers to identify and describe their teaching strategies. In the research project undertaken with six primary teachers cited at the end of Chapter 2 (Anning 1987), two infant teachers commented in detail on the evidence of teaching and learning episodes recorded in their classrooms. They were absolutely clear about why they had used certain strategies. For example a recurrent theme was the need to identify when to intervene directly in children's learning processes and when to hold back from intervention.

One teacher, Wendy, believed that her role was to provide an underlying structure for children's learning. She would therefore deliberately teach technical vocabulary, demonstrate new apparatus to the children, and teach strategies for accessing information from books, dictionaries, textbooks, etc. Sometimes this direct instruction would be as she sat and worked closely with a group, sometimes she would pull the whole class together for a ten-minute burst of direct instruction, and sometimes the instruction would be in the context of an exchange with an individual child engaged on a task. However, she argued that beyond the initial direct guidance she gave, the children should then be encouraged to develop their own strategies for extending that learning.

She was aware that the moment at which the teacher intervened was critical. She described her strategy while working with two very able 6-year-olds on a task which involved them transferring information they had collected about children in the two parallel top infant classes from chart to graph format:

I hadn't used the word graph at any time, but that's what I was trying to get them to do, but I really didn't want to say to them, 'This is how you can make a graph'. I wanted them to try to come to the conclusion themselves that if you're making a graph like that, that you need to do it in a vertical way – to show the difference between each particular thing that you are measuring. And the thing was that I said to them – they put out their cubes horizontally on the table – and I tried to get *them* to make some decision

about placing them in a better way. But it didn't come straight away. So I
didn't – I just left it at that because I didn't want to say, 'Oh no, *this* is the
way you're going to do it.'

When the children obviously hadn't come to what I considered the
right sort of placement for cubes for a graph I just decided to continue.
And I said, 'Oh all right, let's just leave it. We'll talk about that later.' Then
there was quite a bit of silence really because the children did seem to be
working it out for themselves. I chipped in when it wasn't going quite
right.

In another recorded activity, Wendy was working with a mixed ability group of
6–7-year-olds on arranging a list of the names of children in the two top infant
classes into alphabetical order. She described her strategy when the children
first encountered two names beginning with the same letter:

> They found the two names that both began with 'A' and I said, 'Do you
> think it matters where I put them?' I think I was trying to – instead of just
> giving them a rule straight away – I was trying to make them realise the
> *need* for a rule if you know what I mean. In that way they would realise
> that you've got to do something about it – and hopefully they would then
> remember *what* to do about it, rather than just be told. And I wanted them
> to try various strategies themselves, hopefully to see if they could
> somehow get something out of that. You know, to build on what they
> knew and did rather than me just throw in something entirely new to
> them. I wanted *them* really to come up with the answer. I didn't want to
> come in straight away and correct them. Because I've often found that if
> you leave it long enough it evolves anyway; and if it's come from the
> children then they tend to remember it, rather than me, having me tell
> them.

The directive strategies she used were, on the surface, very mechanistic. They
included focusing children's attention on key aspects of learning during the
task. For example commenting on her strategies in the maths activities, she
said:

> I noticed dozens of times I kept recapping on what we'd done before. At
> one point I said to the children, 'Right, let's look what's happening here.'
> Again I brought them back to, 'Now what is it we're trying to show? And
> what are those cubes?' Just so that they would not forget the purpose of
> what we were doing. I came back again with 'What does this cube mean?'
> so that they did understand what we were dealing with. It wasn't a cube as
> a cube. It was just a family. It was representing something else.

This seems to me a perfect illustration of the Donaldson argument that young
children can and should be empowered by adults with access to symbol
systems in the early years of schooling. As Donaldson pointed out, the learning

activities which give opportunities for children to move towards abstractions should be embedded in their realities. In this example, the children were working on a shared, practical activity, dealing with data about their friends in the school, with the skilful 'scaffolding' of a teacher who was concerned to push them towards new levels of intellectual competence.

Another strategy Wendy used was consciously to introduce the children to a new vocabulary of abstractions:

> The word 'represent', now whether they'd come across that before I don't know, but I noticed towards the end of the session I wasn't actually saying, 'What does it mean to you?' I was saying, 'What does it represent?' And they came back with it straight away – so they picked that terminology up.

She also cued children into 'correct' responses when that was necessary to keep the processes and pace of learning moving. In the language activity she explained:

> I did notice my use of inflection when I said to the girls, 'Where are you up to now?' And they said they were up to 'B'. So I said, 'Oh well, what does that mean?' It was quite obvious to anybody listening that what I *did* actually mean was, 'Well, you're nowhere near it yet.' And I presume – I think they did actually pick that up. There were quite a few occasions when it was quite obvious from my voice that they hadn't got the right answer so far.

However, underlying all these basically mechanistic strategies was a constant awareness of the children's likely emotional responses to what she was doing and saying. She knew that she wanted children to develop independence in learning situations, and in order to become independent they had to become confident enough to tackle new learning activities, and she was able to identify clearly the key strategies she used to create an atmosphere in the classroom where the children would 'have a go' without fear of failure. For example she used facial expressions and body language to communicate her support, particularly when children appeared to be anxious:

> I noticed I smiled a lot at them. It must have been quite early in the recording, I think Shane was in the middle of explaining something and I was just nodding and smiling as if to say, 'Yes, you're on the right track. Go on,' because he's quite nervous really, Shane, and he needs that sort of thing. . . .
>
> I did in fact sit quite close to Tom. I normally sit close to the one who needs my physical presence really – I actually put my arm round him.

She used humour to diffuse tension, particularly to support children who were struggling to find the solution to a problem or who had made an obvious mistake, and she treated children in quite different ways depending on their likely emotional responses to risk situations:

I was worried that John might get a bit upset if I put him under pressure for too long. So when it was his go, I left him for a few minutes. But he just wasn't moving at all. His hand was frozen over the shapes. Then I felt I didn't want to embarrass him any more, so I said, 'Do you want to do it or do you want me to help?' Perhaps left he could have done it – but the situation at that point seemed too much. On reflection, I think it was the only thing to do. Looking back it didn't appear to do him any harm because when it came to his turn again he went straight in and did it that time. . . .

I did notice that my attitude was not the same to all of them in that I tend to put more pressure on Shane. Where he was trying to explain something at one point, I did say, 'Yes, carry on,' you know, 'Keep going'. Whereas with Tom I'm perhaps more gentle for instance . . . I definitely put more pressure on Shane. He was explaining what he'd done, and I suppose he was under quite a lot of pressure from me to explain correctly what he'd done. It wasn't enough – I didn't just accept that he'd got the answer right – whereas probably had Tom got it right, I'd have shown a lot of pleasure at that. With Shane I felt, 'Yes, OK. You've got it right but . . .' He needed – was able – to explain it as well. And therefore I expected him to do that for me. . . . Another thing, I noticed when I gave the task to Shane I said, 'I'd like you to do this . . . blah, blah, blah', but when I asked Tom to do a task I said (softening her voice), 'Would you like to . . . ?' which was again this slightly kid glove attitude I've got towards Tom. I suppose it's all the time, you know, giving him encouragement. My interaction with Tom was very gentle all the time.

What these extracts from an experienced infant teacher's account of her strategies demonstrate is that there are many layers of meanings underpinning the minute-by-minute decisions she is making in the classroom. Research which simply records teacher actions using a coding system, or defines teacher strategies simply on the basis of an analysis of transcripts of their talk, or relies on questioning teachers about their intentions and actions without constant reference to real classroom episodes against which to compare their explanations – all these approaches to understanding classroom processes give only partial information. The complexity of teacher decision-making is illustrated in Figure 2 (p. 44) and to slice across the layers of teacher theory and beliefs, teacher planning and teachers' interactive thoughts and decisions at any one point gives a distorted view of the way in which skilful teachers operate in action. But the problem is that working intensively with teachers in order to encourage them to articulate their multiple realities is very time-consuming and expensive. It also requires trust between the observer and the observed, and researchers have to work hard to establish that kind of trust against a history of the teachers' resentment of the negative feedback they have suffered from 'top down' research programmes in the past.

What is also clear is that there *are* patterns common to infant teachers' strategies. Once they have become aware of these patterns, research findings have more chance of 'getting under their skin'. In my experience it is only then that teachers begin to turn to theoretical models with much more commitment to make sense of them.

Models of pedagogy

Jerome Bruner's *Towards a Theory of Instruction* (1966) still seems to provide a useful and usable model of pedagogy for teachers. What is particular about Bruner's work is that he argues his thesis through from an analysis of children's learning, to a model of classroom pedagogy and then to a curriculum framework.

He sees children's learning as moving between three modes of representation: enactive, iconic and symbolic – knowing something through doing it, through a picture or image of it, and through some such symbolic means as language; and all learners move from one mode to another throughout their lives. He argues that the child should be active in discovering important principles – such as the ability to classify and generalize – from practical examples.

> Mastery of the fundamental ideas of a field involves not only the grasping of general principles, but also the development of an attitude toward learning and inquiry, toward guesses and hunches, toward the possibility of solving problems on one's own. . . . To instill such attitudes by teaching requires . . . a sense of excitement about discovery – discovery of regularities of previously unrecognized relations and similarities between ideas, with a resulting sense of self-confidence in one's abilities.
> (Bruner 1960: 20)

> For if we do nothing else we should somehow give to children a respect for their own powers of thinking, for their power to generate good questions, to come up with interesting informed guesses . . . to make . . . study more rational, more amenable to the use of the mind in the large rather than mere memorizing.
> (Bruner 1966: 96)

The role of the teacher is to 'scaffold' the child's learning by gearing the activities, resources and interactions to the level of competence and maturity of the child. The teacher must constantly revisit ideas, spiralling upwards to build endlessly on children's previous understanding, and must, therefore, be aware of what learning the child brings to a task. Bruner argued that 'much of what we do and say in school only makes children feel that they don't know things that in fact they knew perfectly well before we began to talk about them.'

Tizard and Hughes (1984) give a perfect example of this unproductive kind of strategy in *Young Children Learning*. A 4-year-old child, June, approached her teacher with a piece of paper:

Child: Can you cut that in half? Cut it in half?
Teacher: What would you like me to do with it?
Child: Scissors.
Teacher: With the scissors? (Child nods.) Well, you go and get them, will you?
Child: Where are they?
Teacher: Have a look round. (Child goes over to the cupboard, gets some scissors.) Where do you want me to cut it?
Child: There.
Teacher: Show me again, 'cause I don't quite know where the cut's got to go. (Child shows the teacher where she wants the paper cut.) Down there? (Child nods; teacher cuts child's piece of paper in half.) How many have you got now?
Child: (No reply)
Teacher: How many have you got?
Child: (No reply)
Teacher: How many pieces of paper have you got?
Child: Two.
Teacher: Two. What have I done if I've cut it down the middle?
Child: Two pieces.
Teacher: I've cut it in . . . ? (Wants child to say 'half'.)
Child: (No reply)
Teacher: What have I done?
Child: (No reply)
Teacher: Do you know? (Child shakes head.)
Other child: Two.
Teacher: Yes, I've cut it in two. But . . . I wonder, can you think?
Child: In the middle.
Teacher: I've cut it in the middle. I've cut it in *half*! There you are, now you've got two.

(Tizard and Hughes 1984: 194–5)

This transcript also illustrates the 'flatness' of dialogue which characterized many of the nursery class conversations recorded by the Tizard and Hughes team. Teachers dominated talk, simply by the sheer volume and length of utterances they contributed to the 'conversations'. Their talk was also characterized by a string of questions – a 'teaching' device intended to stimulate thinking.

Questioning has been a habitual teaching device since Socrates recommended it, and most of us can remember the agony of trying to monitor, under stern directions from tutors on our teaching practices, which of our questions to children were 'open' and therefore 'appropriate' or 'closed' and 'inappropriate'! Such superficial analysis is unhelpful. It is possible to ask open questions in a decidedly closed way, or closed questions in a way that requires the respondent to think in a divergent way. In the Tizard and Hughes study the teachers' questions seemed to be designed either to assess at a very simple level what the child already knew – 'What colour is your jersey?' – or to promote their linguistic or cognitive competence – 'What do you think will happen if we plant these seeds?' But the conversation between June and her teacher illustrates the dangers inherent in this approach to teaching young children. The child, as Bruner suggested often happens in schools, is made to 'feel that they don't know things that in fact they knew perfectly well'. June had asked her teacher to cut the paper 'in half' in her initiating turn in the conversation. From the moment of initiation her contributions to the talk were reduced by the teacher's style of interaction, designed to elicit the 'correct' answer (which June had in fact already given), to one- or two-word utterances. Such exchanges clearly do not empower children with 'a respect for their own powers of thinking'. If the emphasis is genuinely to be on 'starting where the child is' teachers must learn to listen to children and engage in dialogue rather than cross examination.

Teacher as agent of control

The teacher's view

In order to function as instructors it is inevitable that teachers exercise some form of control over the social behaviour of children in their classrooms. For many teachers, trained in the traditions of child-centredness, there are real dilemmas presented by the control of children in reconciling the needs of the individual with the needs of the class. Teachers set a high value on the quality of their relationships with pupils as individuals, but in organizing all the children into routines which allow teaching to take place, they are forced to coerce individual children into 'norms' of acceptable school behaviour. The profound uneasiness which teachers feel about this dichotomy is often expressed at the end of the first week of infant school teaching practice when idealistic postgraduate students, white-faced and exhausted, will blurt out, 'I don't want to behave like a dictator or policeman! But that's exactly what I hear myself doing.' They have, in their naivety, identified a critical issue – the potential abuse of power that is inherent in teacher–pupil relationships in schools. In order to reconcile the uneasiness they feel about the unequal power relationship, experienced teachers of young children moderate the exercise of their power by clearly identifiable strategies designed to soften the processes of establishing their authority.

The child's experience

Recent studies of the 'rites of passage' as children make the transition from home to school have highlighted some of the inevitable discontinuities in their experiences of home and school life. Barrett (1986), in a report on the responses of reception class children to school commissioned by the Assistant Masters and Mistresses Association, described the difficulties children beginning school have in coming to terms with rituals such as milktime, playtime, procedures for going to the toilet, lining up and assemblies. For young children used to operating within the easy-going routines of home or playgroup, these are mysterious rites – and adults rarely explain to them *why* they should conform to the novel patterns of behaviour required of them. They may also find some of the classroom activities somewhat bizarre. What sense can a young child make, for example, of being offered a waist-high container of sand or water, assorted containers, a command to put on a mysterious garment described as an apron, and a constant rhetorical question '*How* many children are allowed in the sand/water?' whenever they set out intrepidly across the classroom to join in the ritual? Most significantly, children have to learn how to operate as one of a large group of people when their previous experiences may have been limited to socializing only with small groups of family or friends.

A more extensive study of the transition from home to school (Cleave *et al.* 1982) which formed one part of a National Foundation for Educational Research project, 'Continuity of Children's Experience in the Years 3 to 8', looked at the 'sources of shock' experienced by children entering sixty-three infant classes from a range of pre-school settings: childminders, playgroups, day nurseries, nursery classes and schools. The study identified potential sources of shock as:

1 The setting – the scale of the building, the range of movement required by access to toilets, school hall, playground, etc., and the constraints on the child's movement around his or her own classroom territory.
2 The curriculum – the daily programme, the range of activities, the amount of choice the child has in how to spend his or her time.
3 The people – contact with older, bigger and noisier children (particularly on the school playground), competition for teacher attention, organizational constraints imposed by unfamiliar adults such as welfare assistants, teachers on playground duty or the headteacher.

The team concluded:

Three ingredients are essential if shock is to be reduced to a minimum:

1 Changes and the introduction of new experiences must be *gradual* rather than sudden.
2 People, places and things must to some extent be *familiar* rather than totally strange.
3 The child must have a sense of *security* rather than instability

(Cleave *et al.* 1982: 210)

The teacher's role in the socialization of pupils

What then are the processes by which teachers socialize young children into acceptable school behaviour? King (1978) described some of them in his wry account of life in infant school classrooms. He based his descriptions on observations in three infant schools over a three-year period. The children came to know him as 'The Man in the Wendy House'! He described the strategies the teachers used to impose their middle-class cultural views of appropriate school interests and behaviours on their school populations, while at the same time preserving their 'ideology' of the innocence of childhood.

> Their methods of control were typically oblique, particularly with younger children. Their preference was to make requests rather than to give orders, to reward good behaviour rather than punish the bad. These actions were consonant with the idea of the children being innocent. They were capable of being naughty but did not have naughty intentions. When I put this analysis to teachers they confirmed it with phrases like, 'Well, yes, you can't really blame them, can you?'
>
> (King 1978: 50)

The teachers monitored children's behaviour by constantly scanning the classroom and making eye-contact with or directing disapproving looks at children who were stepping out of line. They also used 'public and private voices' to exercise control. A public comment like, 'I can see a group over there not working', would have a 'ripple' effect on other children in the classroom, as would specific comments to a child such as, 'Have you put the date on your paper, Paul?' Reference control was used when some external authority was invoked. Typical invocations would be, 'Now, nice and quietly down the corridor. You know Mrs Brown [the headteacher] does not like noisy children', or 'Put the apron on. What would Mummy say if you come home with paint on that nice new jumper?' Sometimes control was couched in a game, 'Boys close eyes. Girls creep out, quietly get your coats. Don't let the boys hear you!', or a mechanistic quietening-down routine, 'Hands on heads. Fingers on lips. Lock hands in laps.' Private voices were used when an individual child or small group were being addressed and were generally much softer in tone as well as volume.

In order to impose classroom rules, the teachers discouraged behaviour that was labelled 'silly' and rewarded children for being 'sensible'. King quotes typical teacher comments which made their frames of reference explicit through the use of well-chosen adjectives and adverbs:

> Now I can see the *sensible* people because they are *busy* working already.
>
> Go into prayers *quietly* and *sensibly*, sing as *nicely* as you can.
> I want Paul to sit by me because he has been so *nice* and *helpful*.
> Gary you are being *silly* and *noisy*. No, I'm not smiling, I'm sorry.

Politeness was insisted upon:

Boy: Can I go to the toilet?
Teacher: Pardon? (She has heard what he said.)
Child: Can I go to the toilet, please?
Teacher: Just remember those two very special words.
Children: (in chorus) Please and thankyou.

The processes of peer group socialization

Jane, the second infant teacher in Anning's research project (Anning 1988), was aware of the value of particular children with high peer group status in supporting her control strategies in the classroom. She described the behaviour of a child whom she had taught previously in the nursery, and who now formed part of a reception class:

> I recognise – I think it's perhaps because I've taught him for two years – I recognise Christian's phrasing in mine. Particularly in the classroom. And I can hear – it's almost that he's saying the word, but when I'm just sort of thinking it – but it's the word I want to use, you know. . . . It's happened since we've been doing 'time', and Christian has picked up on it even more. We can go into PE and they'll be half an hour for PE. They've five pieces of apparatus to go on if they're all doing their tasks properly and not being silly. And we have gone into the hall when it's taken a long time for them all to get changed, a long time to line up, being silly in the line, silly in the hall – and they've probably done two pieces of apparatus and Christian has then said, 'You know *why?*' to them 'Because now we've only got . . .' and he's the first one to look at the clock now when we go into the hall. He'll say, 'Look, we've got to be quick because we're late coming in because we've been silly', you know, he's worked it all out. And gradually more and more are beginning to do it and become aware of it. That's – I feel they've learnt a lot.

Jane was honest enough to admit that she used a form of emotional blackmail as one of her range of control strategies:

> The only time I deliberately make the children feel uncomfortable is when they are behaving objectionably. And then they know who they are, and I do it then for a different reason – so that I can get them to modify their behaviour so they can have me, Mrs H, as she is when they are behaving normally. When they are behaving in an objectionable way, then they must do something to get me to be *nice*. And I only need a facial gesture some time. I don't need to use words.

In turn those same key children, who knew Jane's moods, would try to prevent this uncomfortable tension in the classroom from surfacing;

Christian, when I begin to do that, when he sees this thing of me falling apart, will say loudly, 'This is ridiculous, you're all being very silly, aren't they, Miss?' And he'll spell it out before it happens. And then one or two others will pick the cues up – and gradually they do it for me – and I don't have to do anything except stand and look disapproving.

The linguistic conventions of control

Mary Willes (1983) describes the highly specific uses of language associated with establishing classroom routines. These rule-governed language conventions have to be learned by the young child. The structures reflect the power vested in the adult position of authority and, because they then transfer to teaching and learning episodes, form a substantial obstacle to the kind of 'open' dialogue that characterizes the pedagogy Bruner suggests is conducive to encouraging children to be confident and independent learners. The teacher sees her role as keeping the discourse flowing. She has the right to decide on changes of subject, to interrupt children, to ignore inappropriate contributions. Children learn that they are expected to provide brief responses (particularly in so-called class 'discussions') so that others do not get fidgety; to keep silent in teaching situations unless nominated or invited to bid for teacher attention; and to try to make guesses to get as near as possible to the 'correct' answer in the teacher's head when they are asked a direct question. Sinclair and Coulthard (1975), who designed a model of discourse analysis for classrooms, asked 'How does the five year old who speaks when he wants to become the ten year old who waits to be nominated?' If the conventions described by Willes are established at the point when children are at their most vulnerable, as 'relatively inexperienced members of the speech community', that is at point of entry to school, it is not surprising that when teachers attempt at a later date in junior or secondary classes to get children to negotiate for a more 'equal' pattern of discourse, the children are resistant to change. The same patterns even persist into higher education where in seminars or tutorials students assume that tutors will sustain the dialogue, and tutors, socialized into distrust of silences, will 'fill up the vacancies of attention', with instructional talk.

Nor is it surprising that attempts to elicit children's views of the role of the teacher have confirmed that they are very much aware of the power of teachers as authority figures. Willes (1983) tried initially to elicit children's views about how they perceived the relations between teacher and taught, and their grasp of the linguistic conventions that expressed those relationships, by observing them in free play with a Fisher Price Playschool. The children did tend to play out 'school routines' like registration with the four small pupil and one teacher doll. However, to gain more systematic information, Willes designed a storybook, illustrated by photographs, of some normal events in a morning at school. The children were asked to fill in gaps, in an oral or written cloze procedure, at various points in the book. Over the time-span of three terms, it was clear that the children were increasingly aware of the school routines and accompanying conventions of school talk. In adjusting or 'settling down' to school, they had learned 'to accept their place as very junior members of an elaborate social hierarchy' (Newson and Newson 1977: 45).

Young children also quickly pick up on 'fear of wrong doing' in this hierarchical school culture. When Barrett used a similar technique of showing 5-year-olds a series of photographs of classroom events during their first few weeks in school, their responses indicated dependency and anxiety:

> Girls can't do it – perhaps she's drawing a ship.

> A boy doesn't know what to do. He is sucking his pencil. He cannot do his work. He must tell his teacher.

> I don't know how to do it – I didn't know how to paint or mix the colours properly.

> I didn't like to write when I came to school. I couldn't make a snail. I couldn't draw a picture. It was too hard. I was too little.

> I feel miserable when I can't do it. I'm frightened I might get it wrong.

These fears were expressed by children whose teachers had tried hard to make the transition to school a happy experience – by staggering the school entry, starting children off on part-time attendance, involving parents closely in the initial entry to school. Yet the children still felt anxious about the demands of the school activities. It is sobering evidence of the children's distress and worrying when we know that learning is not likely to be effective when the learner feels stressed or anxious.

Pupil power

However, power is not solely vested in the adult in the classroom. Andrew Pollard (1985; 1988) has provided some fascinating analyses of the power of children's culture in primary classrooms. He argues that children are not nearly as passive in the negotiation of classroom processes as has been suggested in previous studies of classroom life.

> Child culture and child friendship groups generate norms, values, rules, understandings and a sense of social structure which is extremely complex and sophisticated ... and these provide a means by which children make sense of and cope with the adult world when it impinges on them.
>
> (Pollard 1985: 245)

Pollard argues that both the pupils and the teacher have dominant 'interests at hand'. Figure 3 indicates what these interests are.

He argues that the teacher and the children negotiate, from their

Teachers   *Children*
SELF ←————————————————→ SELF
- self-image   - self-image
- workload   - enjoyment
- health and stress   - control of stress
- enjoyment   - retention of dignity
- autonomy

ORDER ←————————————————→ PEER GROUP MEMBERSHIP

INSTRUCTION ←————————————————→ LEARNING

Figure 3   Primary and enabling interests of teachers and children
Source: Pollard 1985: 156

standpoints of different concerns and interests, towards a 'working consensus'. The teacher will negotiate for acceptable noise levels, attention to tasks, movement around the classroom, clearing up the classroom – while the children will negotiate for time to 'easy ride', legitimate reasons for moving around the classroom to talk to friends (pencil sharpening is a favourite ploy), avoidance of tidying up activities ('Miss, can I go to the toilet? I'm *desperate*'). Most children are willing to comply with the working consensus – they do not particularly like hassle – though some children may challenge the system either by subtle strategies of evasion or by overt rebellion. These isolated instances of deviance will be explained away by teachers as a child who is 'going through a phase', possibly because of some trouble at home, or the result of immaturity, 'something he'll grow out of', or in extreme cases as a child beyond the normal range of 'naughtiness' expected in classrooms and therefore referable to the educational psychologist. But the combined power of a class of children, who have decided to reject a teacher's authority because they are bored, frustrated or angered by his or her behaviour, can be very effective. It can drive a supply teacher out of the school after one day, never to return, or devastate an inexperienced student; and, of course, it is fear that they will not be able to cope with the combined power of their pupils that makes student teachers resort to 'policeman' or 'dictator' tactics.

In Nias' sample of six experienced teachers, on the other hand, it was significant that they claimed that they were able to work in a collaborative rather than authoritative way with pupils only when they felt 'relaxed', 'easy', 'not frightened any more', 'able to be themselves'. 'In other words a classroom climate in which teachers feel secure appears to be a necessary condition for the establishment of self-directed, purposeful learning on the part of the pupils' (Nias 1988: 133). The task for teachers is to negotiate a climate where they can talk openly and honestly with children about the need for shared responsibility for the mechanics of managing and organizing a classroom, for getting through a reasonable amount of work each day, for having fun, for admitting when things have gone wrong. Lynne, one of the teachers in Nias' sample, wrote:

> What teaching this way means for me is that I'm happy. I feel cared for. I don't feel as if I'm acting. I don't feel stressed or bored. I never look at the clock. I don't have to fight for control – and I have the satisfaction of knowing that I do the job better, that I'm a better teacher. . . . I expect it to be a two-way thing – for example, if I've been away ill, I want them to ask me how I am. . . . If I think they're trying it on, I'll tell them why I think it's crappy. . . It's important that they do something as well as they can, then they can get the satisfaction from it. It's *their* work but I tell them what I think about it.

> (Nias 1988: 135)

We need studies of classrooms where this kind of working consensus between the teacher and the children has been achieved – where children are producing high standards of work and where teachers are functioning effectively. What is clear is that infant teachers cannot operate a pedagogy which is based on principles which encourage children to take responsibility for their own learning if they at the same time are discouraging children from taking responsibility for their own behaviour.

Teacher as respondent to external pressures

Societal and cultural values and teachers

Teachers bring to the classroom a set of values that have been acquired from their own personal histories as well as from the professional contexts in which they have worked. The values they hold have a profound influence on their behaviour as teachers (see Figure 1, p. 18). It has already been suggested that a particular type of person enters the teaching profession. Most teachers' family backgrounds are middle class or skilled working class, though of course their subsequent careers, personal situations, or higher education may have broadened their life experiences. Nevertheless, there is evidence that teachers present a set of values and aspirations to pupils which reflect white, British, middle-class assumptions, even when they are at pains to prevent this happening.

In the 1970s and 1980s a series of studies in primary schools identified aspects of teachers' attitudes towards class and race, and more recently towards gender, which affect the way teachers behave towards children.

Class

Nash (1973) addressed the 'expectancy' problem (research reviewed in Pilling and Kellmer Pringle 1978: Part IV), which had become a key issue in educational research in the vanguard of destreaming in primary schools and the transition from selective to comprehensive secondary education. His concern was to explore how far teachers' attitudes towards their pupils influenced pupil self-concept and performance in schools. He worked with eight junior school teachers and from them elicited the most common constructs they held about their pupils as learners – hardworking/lazy, mature/immature, and well-behaved/poorly behaved. He then observed interactions between the teachers and their pupils, and it was clear that the teachers treated the children differently according to their perceptions of them. The evidence upon which the teachers made their judgements was not always accurate. In some instances, for example, the teachers wrongly attributed children to a particular social background. Slower and less likeable children were perceived as coming from poor homes, though objective data indicated that their background was similar to other well-regarded children in the class. The teachers claimed that they 'knew each child well', but 'knowing' in this sense appeared to be very much within the school context and cultural expectations. The teachers also claimed that they were scrupulously fair and treated all pupils the same. Nash's evidence suggested that teachers clearly preferred some children above others, and their behaviour towards them reflected their preferences.

Another study was carried out with the headteacher and infant staff of a primary school by Sharp and Green (1975). They explored the gap between the 'theories' of progressivism implicit in the teachers' talk and the realities of their classroom practice. They found that teachers spent more time interacting with the 'ideal' pupils who were usually defined as coming from 'good homes'. Their success as effective 'progressive' teachers was measured against these successful school learners' progress. On the other hand failure to learn was attributed to 'bad home backgrounds' rather than to factors within school. Ironically the children who were most in need of direct teacher attention were most likely to be sent off to play or to practical activities to keep themselves occupied until they were 'ready' to learn. Thus the gap between those succeeding and those failing on school tasks began to widen.

King (1978) found that teachers' assessment and typification of pupils were based on three aspects of pupil behaviour – their compliance with teacher rules, their relationship with other children and their progress in learning – but in making judgements teachers were also influenced by assumptions about children's home backgrounds. The way they interacted with pupils was profoundly influenced by these typifications. Thus King wrote,

> The posing of the family–home background theory was made easier, if not actually made possible, by their child-centred practices, which presented them with the 'evidence' of the children's homes and families through their writing, drawing and talking. Taking an interest in the whole child legitimated knowing about his or her life outside the

classroom. Thus the child-centredness permitted the family–home background theory and was protected by it.

(King 1978: 146)

The deficit view of working-class children had been legitimized in the massive programmes of compensatory education in the 1960s (see Chapter 1). In the 1970s the spectre of teacher expectations determining pupil progress loomed large and at the same time the myths about 'working-class' homes being without books, culture or indeed 'language' began to be dispelled. Yet there is worrying evidence that teachers continue to make judgements about pupils based on sketchy understanding of their home backgrounds. It is also clear that the judgements are not simply based on assumptions about class, but are the result of a subtle and complex interplay of attitudes towards class, race and gender. These attitudes affect the way in which teachers respond to pupils in classrooms, and this in turn affects the way pupils perceive themselves as 'good' or 'bad' pupils and as successful or unsuccessful learners.

Race
Research into teachers' attitudes towards race have shown marginal changes in the past decade. In Elaine Brittan's (1976) study of 500 teachers in 25 primary and secondary schools, where the school population of ethnic minority children ranged from 18 per cent to 24 per cent, 94 per cent of the teachers claimed to support the principle that 'schools have a responsibility to promote good race relations among pupils'. They agreed that assemblies and religious education syllabuses should reflect minority faiths, and that some curriculum changes should be made to accommodate the countries of origin of ethnic minority children.

However, many also expressed a strongly assimilationist line, claiming that 'immigrant children should merge in with the English pupils'. Little and Willey's *Studies in the Multi-Ethnic Curriculum* (1983) reported that most teachers were impatient with the small but vociferous lobby of professionals committed to multi-cultural education for all schools. They saw the issues as 'irrelevant both to them and to their pupils'. Teacher attitudes displayed 'the whole gamut of racial misunderstandings and folk mythology ... racial stereotypes were common and attitudes ranged from the unveiled hostility of few, through the apathy of many and the condescension of others, to total acceptance by a minority.' In the 1970s and 1980s pressure began to grow from minority groups to examine the possible effects of negative teacher attitudes and low expectations on black children's school achievement. In 1979 the government set up a Committee of Inquiry into the Education of Children from Ethnic Minority Groups. The Rampton Report (DES 1981b), *West Indian Children in Our Schools*, was published in 1981, followed by the Swann Report in 1985, from which this extract is taken:

It will be evident that society is faced with a dual problem: eradicating the discriminatory attitudes of the white majority on the one hand, and on the other, evolving an educational system which ensures that *all* pupils achieve their full potential.

(Swann Committee 1985: 2.6, 768)

Gender

During the 1980s attention was focused on the differential treatment of girls and boys in classrooms. The Sex Discrimination Act 1975 included education in its scope, and the Equal Opportunities Commission was set up to monitor the principles of 'equality of opportunity' for all. Local authorities have responded by producing guidelines on equal opportunities. But paper policies never quite match up to classroom realities, and research has identified some crucial differences in the way in which teachers perceive boys and girls and the way in which they interact with them (Clarricoates 1980; Spender 1982; Whyte 1983; Weiner 1985; Mullin *et al.* 1987). Teachers differentiate between girls and boys in control and organizational strategies. Competition between boys and girls is encouraged by infant teachers as a way of urging children to work harder or behave better. Registers are called separately; boys and girls are expected to line up separately; to wash their hands separately; sometimes to play in separate school playgrounds.

There is plenty of evidence that boys dominate teacher time and talk. When Dale Spender tried to compensate for this known imbalance by deliberately trying to distribute her attention evenly between girls and boys, in ten taped lessons with secondary age children,

the maximum time I spent interacting with girls was 42% and on average 38%, and the minimum time with boys was 58%. It is nothing short of a substantial shock to appreciate the discrepancy between what I *thought* I was doing and what I actually *was* doing.

(Spender 1982: 56)

Most infant teachers are equally shocked when they realize, through observations or the use of tape recordings, how boys dominate classroom talk. Despite the fact that adult power is held by a predominantly female work-force in infant schools, boys learn how to dominate favoured 'male' space and resources such as computers and brick play, outdoor equipment, and key playground areas.

From the outset of schooling, girls are orientated towards the demands of the teacher, rather than the task. While boys seek attention through aggression and rule-breaking, girls seek approval through conforming to pupil norms. Although girls' intellectual achievement is in general better than that of boys, they retreat from sex-competition, lack confidence and react more negatively to perceived failure. They comply with the male orientation of resources, tasks and norms and in doing so 'learn to lose'.

(Whyte 1983: 32)

It is, however, also true that boys receive far more negative feedback from their teachers. This may explain in part why more boys than girls demonstrate aggression and deviance throughout the school system. If you are constantly being reprimanded publicly for noise, movement around the classroom, and aggressive behaviour, it seems likely that you will assume that these character-istics are expected of you by teachers and will oblige with the appropriate behaviours. It is also self-evident that not all boys conform to the 'macho' stereotype; nor that all girls conform to the stereotype of passive compliance. The attempt by a team of researchers from Northern Ireland (Mullin *et al.* 1987) to explore categories of 'visible' and 'invisible' children in infant classrooms, and only within that overall system to begin to locate gender differences in behaviours, seems a more promising approach.

Effects of teacher expectation on pupil progress

Most teachers feel guilty when they become aware of research findings into the 'self-fulfilling' prophecies of teacher expectations and pupil progress. They have learnt to adopt self-censoring strategies when they talk publicly about issues of race, class and gender. For example the label 'working class' is more often substituted by euphemisms such as 'does not have a supportive home', though in fairness to teachers this has been demonstrated to be a more tangible source of determining school failure than generalizations made on the basis of parental occupations and income.

Where is the hard evidence of the effect on pupil progress of infant teachers', often unconsciously, classist, racist, and sexist attitudes? In their study of thirty-three ILEA infants schools, Tizard *et al.* (1988) tried to tease out the effects of home background, parental aspirations and teacher attitudes on the school progress of working-class white and Afro-Caribbean boys and girls. Attainments at school entry were highly predictive of attainments at the end of infant schooling. The factors at home which appeared to influence attainment at school entry were parents' educational qualifications and the amount they helped children with school work at home, particularly the experience they gave children of books. Over three years black boys made the least progress in reading, and black girls the most progress. Boys made more progress in maths.

The effect of teacher and school factors was much less clear. The team hedge their findings with caveats, but they acknowledge that

> teachers' expectations and the range of children's curriculum coverage, and, to a lesser extent, whether children were seen to have behaviour problems, to be under-achieving, and to be a pleasure to teach, were associated with children's school attainment and progress. Teacher expectations and curriculum coverage were themselves associated, and it was suggested that the range of curriculum coverage activities given to

individual children may be one way that teacher's expectations operate in the classroom.

(Tizard *et al.* 1988: 142)

This issue will be explored in the discussion of the infant school curriculum in Chapter 4.

One label that is consistently used by teachers to explain school failure is single-parent status of a child's family. What is the evidence of this link? Osborn and Milbank (1987) examined the effects of changes in home life to which children in the longitudinal Child Health and Education Study were subjected between the ages of 5 and 10 on their educational attainment and behaviour at 10. They concluded that single parent status *per se* did not affect the school progress of the children, though a change for the worse (the continuum being measured from the optimal situation of both natural parents present to the least desirable, from the child's point of view, of the child being placed with foster or grandparents) did increase the risk of conduct disorder and hyperactivity. On the other hand, an increase in family size, especially of two or more children, did reduce a child's test scores. It is important that teachers are made aware of these kinds of data. 'Family' types are as varied as the number of children in a class, and we should be wary of making assumptions about the 'ideal' two-parent, two-children, nuclear family and school success.

Teacher values and controversial issues

It is impossible, perhaps even undesirable, for teachers to be neutral in the values they bring to educating young children. In this sense they are both guilty and innocent. But particularly worrying for nursery and infant staff is how to deal with classroom incidents that reflect children's awareness of complex social problems gained through television news coverage, soap operas like *EastEnders*, videos, newspapers and adult talk. How do teachers deal with ethical and moral issues with young children? There has been little support for teachers in the teaching of moral education and little research into the moral development of children (see pp. 40–41).

In 1986 *Child Education* (Anning *et al.* 1986) funded a small-scale exploratory study of the strategies nursery and infant teachers used when confronted with examples of children playing out, for example violent clashes between police and strikers or miners, teachers' striking, terrorism, overt sexual behaviour, sexist stereotypes, or when children manifested overt racism, religious intolerance or bullying.

The strategies teachers used were categorized as involvement or extension, direction or manipulation, and delay or diversion.

Involvement or extension

In involvement or extension strategies (27 per cent of the total categorized), teachers listened to, joined in with or explored in talk the children's feelings about the incidents without expressing their own views. For example, when the children were playing 'cops' versus miners:

If the children were playing (in a violent way) without involving too many others I might simply join them and listen. After all, this seems to me a clear example of children playing through anxieties. After a while I might add a few things such as, 'Why are you calling the policemen pigs? How do you think they might feel? What do you think the policemen tell their children when they get home?'

When the home corner was a space-ship:

Boy: And I'll be the astronaut. Give me the back-pack. You can't be the astronaut.
Girl: (holding on to it) I am.
Boy: No. . . . You're a girl.
Girl still holds on tightly to the back-pack. At this point I intervened, asking the girl, 'Well, what do you think?' The whole group talked briefly about whether or not girls could be astronauts. 'If nots' had to be justified with 'why nots' and the argument was easily resolved.

Direction or manipulation
In direction or manipulation strategies (41 per cent), teachers made their views very clear, with or without giving reasons, or while appearing to accept children's ideas, gave preference to those which accorded with their own, or manipulated the children's feelings. For example when the children announced they were 'on strike':

I would point out that when in school the teacher works and that as the children are there too they must tidy up otherwise the classroom cannot function. I would not attempt to discuss the politics of strike action with very young children.

When children were heard making racist remarks:

A visitor (coloured) walked into the school and the children aged 6 and 7 years remarked, 'Here's a blackie,' and were generally rude. I dealt with it immediately, quickly and firmly, saying sternly, 'I think you have said some very silly and hurtful things. I don't want to hear anybody say silly things like that again.' I made it clear I strongly disapprove and would not tolerate it.

When the children said they were glad about the bomb planted in a Brighton hotel which had nearly killed Mrs Thatcher:

I asked them, 'How would you feel if your mummy had been bombed?'

Delay or diversion

In delay or diversion strategies (32 per cent), the teacher made no immediate effort to become involved but either ignored the incident or attempted to distract the children's attention. For example when children were simulating sex in the house corner:

> I knocked on the door and said, 'It's Postman Pat. I've got a letter for you.'

When children were making racist remarks in a class discussion:

> I would probably try to ignore 80 per cent of this discussion as too much recognition may encourage more comments.

Individual teachers' strategies

It was difficult to detect consistency in the strategies described by each teacher, because it was clear that the teacher's own value system dictated the response made to each separate incident. However, some teachers offered general views about dealing with controversial issues such as:

> One of the problems in dealing with controversial incidents like this with young children is that most of the time they are echoing views and remarks of parents. One does not want to undermine the stability of home–school relationships but at the same time has to try to broaden the attitudes of children. With older children in primary schools it is possible to encourage independent thought because they already have examples of occasions when they disagree with parents' views. In general, I think one has to act immediately to prevent volatile situations from getting out of hand. But one should also be aware that issues such as racial and gender stereotyping, tolerance and violence should be dealt with in the infant curriculum. I see little educational benefit in the approach voiced in responses such as, 'We don't have that sort of behaviour in this school,' since it is merely pushing the problems out of sight only to re-emerge later.

Other responses were from teachers who, still hanging on to the myth of childhood innocence, appeared to want to do precisely this:

> I think there can be a danger of 'blowing up' casually repeated remarks (heard at home?) to represent an attitude which is clearly not present in the classroom. Mindless comments about ethnic groups copied from an adult could be part of everyday conversation without affecting a younger child's great friendship with a 'Paki' for instance.

It is this sort of ostrich-like response which caused some of the ILEA teachers in Tizard's study to claim that there was no racist behaviour in their schools when the children could describe specific incidents of verbal and physical abuse (see Tizard *et al*. 1988: 157). A more helpful approach is for teachers to face up to the harsh realities of children's lives and provide a supportive and humane climate in which children can begin to establish their own moral framework. Perhaps whole-school approaches can be helpful in establishing some consistency and 'common sense' in dealing with controversial issues, while at the same time allowing for individual differences in values held by staff and pupils. An ILEA infant school headteacher described a 'whole-school' approach to dealing with conflict:

> Our strategies overall to deal with conflict include much work in discussions where children are encouraged to explore conflict, motives, feelings, possible resolutions. Drama is the main teaching strategy which puts children into conflict, problem-solving activities and allows them the safety-net of distance. We have a responsibility to protect a child from racism, sexism, or any name-calling, bullying, etc. We also hope to develop moral awareness using suitable stories – and sometimes 'unsuitable' – for discussion. Conflict in the playground we talk about extensively. The school has adopted two key words, 'caring and sharing', to particularly be aware of when in their playground space. We have a positive policy for aggression problems and this has been blessed by parents. Nearly 100 attended a meeting this term to discuss the policy and add to it, and to bless the built-in deterrents. The parents discussed their difficulties of telling children to 'hit back', especially when they played out (holidays, evenings, etc.). We talked about the fact that children and adults accept different 'rules' in different situations and they could recognize that at school certain 'rules' may be acceptable that seem unacceptable at home. I'm not happy that children should hit back when playing out, but there is a line when 'Home rules OK', and I am simply not able to support the children out of school. One can hope that 'school' values in this case might develop at home.

The final sentences of this statement make an important point. Teachers cannot be expected to set the world right in the face of societal pressures. However, they *may* be expected to be aware of the need to offer alternative models of moral frameworks to children. I would also argue that they *must* be aware of how their own value systems can operate, perhaps unconsciously, to the detriment of children's progress in school.

There is a woeful lack of in-service work devoted to this vital area of teachers' professional development. A final comment from a teacher who responded to the *Child Education* survey expresses with clarity the difficulty many teachers feel:

> So much is dependent on the ethos of the school and the relationship with parents which is built up over a long period. It is important that children feel secure in knowing there is room for many views. The teacher is more of a mediator and must never press their own views in the

classroom but act as a catalyst in order that children have opportunities to mature in play, discussions and living together in a unity which allows for differences. The humanity of everyone must be accepted – including the teacher. We're all fallible.

I have an overall high level of concern about the decline of real values in society (social, moral and spiritual), and particularly how politicians and top powers seem to have double standards in these areas. This presents educators with a problem. To many children real care and empathy can be a new experience – to some a completely 'foreign language'.

Teacher strategies and the curriculum

As we have seen from the issues explored in this chapter, the strategies used by infant teachers are underpinned by multiple layers of thinking and feeling. It is particularly galling when this kind of practical intelligence is undervalued within the teaching profession. But the responsibility for redressing the Joyce Grenfell image must lie partly with the teachers who work with young children. The teachers quoted in this chapter have begun the demanding process of articulating their thinking.

Equally demanding for teachers is the ability to define the curriculum they offer to 4–8-year-olds in a way which is rigorous but at the same time genuinely compatible with their preferred ways of working in classrooms. The infant school curriculum will be the focus of the next chapter.

4

The curriculum

The curriculum is one of those slippery words, like 'the integrated day' or 'group work', that are widely used by educators but often mean different things to different users. In this chapter the word will be used in the broad sense that John Kerr defined it as 'all the learning which is planned and guided by the school, whether it is carried on in groups or individually, inside or outside the school' (Kerr 1968: 16). Discussion of the curriculum in infant schools will be grouped under the following headings: 'The organization of the classroom', 'The structuring of learning in the school day' and 'The content of the curriculum'.

The organization of the classroom

The physical layout

The physical layout of most classrooms in infant schools in the UK conforms to a recognizable pattern. There will be a carpeted area which often doubles as the book corner and the site for registration, whole-class instruction, stories, etc. There will be curriculum 'areas' more or less identifiable, either through the storage of 'subject' specific resources or, more emphatically, by workshop-type spaces, for maths, language and 'messy' activities. Tables will be grouped together, usually scattered around the middle area of the classroom, to allow for groups of up to six to eight children to sit together for 'seat work'. There may also be 'play' areas such as the house corner, a carpeted area for construction play, and sand and water containers. There will probably be an interest table reflecting the current theme chosen by the teacher as the focus for topic work, and the classroom displays of children's work, predominantly art based, will also reflect that topic. Other teacher-produced wall displays will serve a didactic purpose: a number line in the maths area, lists of the most commonly used words for the children's writing activities in the language area, a *Child Education* poster related to the current topic.

The physical layouts of classrooms have reflected the beliefs and ideologies that infant teachers espouse and assumptions about 'best practice' as defined by successive official documents such as the Hadow Report (Board of Education 1931), the Plowden Report (CACE 1967) and the HMI surveys of primary schools (DES 1978a; 1982a). Golby (1988) describes classrooms as the 'curriculum in waiting'.

> What is in the classroom, and where it is, is so in every case for a reason, or set of reasons. Like the classroom itself, a human invention that came into being at a certain time through an act of educational imagination.
>
> (Golby 1988: 28)

The practical areas are there because teachers believe that children learn by doing. The tables are pushed together because children should work in groups, not as a class. The displays are there because they are said to reflect what is currently 'turning the children on'. The messages are as clear as those announced by the rows of uniform desks facing the blackboard at the front, and the imposing teacher's desk raised high on a platform, of the elementary school classroom.

But what is really happening when teachers and pupils are functioning as teacher and taught in the kinds of physical contexts described? Close observation of the use of the infant classroom environment, set out like a stall for learning, will probably reveal that areas are used rather differently from the way the rhetoric would lead one to expect. It is likely that the book corner is rarely used by the children as a space for quiet and sustained reading (Southgate *et al.* 1981). Instead the comfortable carpet is likely to provide the boundaries for wriggling children at story-times or the ubiquitous 'mat' time when they are awaiting instructions for the next session. The house corner or, in some cases, the 'messy' areas may be out of bounds for children until after dinner and may therefore remain empty around the periphery for long periods of the day while children squeeze themselves into a crowded middle area of the classroom getting on with the 'real' work of the basics. As for the children working together in groups, the evidence is that group work is very rare in junior (Galton *et al.* 1980) or infant classrooms (N. Bennett *et al.* 1984).

Observations of where the teacher spends most time will probably identify that he or she is based predominantly in the middle area of the classroom where the 'seat-based' work takes place, making occasional brief forays into the play and practical areas. Non-teaching assistants – parents, nursery nurses, secondary school pupils on 'Life Skills' placements – reverse this pattern of movement. There may be then a bleak picture of mismatch between the physical manifestations of the stated intentions of infant teachers in the layout of the classroom, and the realities of how the learning environment is actually used.

The Primary Needs Independent Evaluation Project (1986–90), based at the University of Leeds, focused in one of their formative evaluation reports on the Leeds City Council funded Primary Needs Programme on classroom organization (Evaluation Report Ten, *Changing Classroom Practice: Decisions and Dilemmas*, reported in Prindep 1989 and in Alexander *et al*. 1989: 239–300). The report surveyed the physical arrangements and management of learning in the classrooms of thirty-eight primary teachers and monitored their responses to an LEA course on 'good practice' in classroom organization and layout. The LEA policy was defined as 'flexible teaching strategies within a quality environment rich in stimulus and challenge'. A detailed study of the classrooms, beliefs and practices of ten of the teachers provides some useful information on the variety of ways in which teachers organize their classrooms as well as how they respond to prescriptions about 'good practice'.

Mrs C was teaching twenty-seven 5–6-year-olds. Her classroom had labelled storage spaces for maths equipment, text books, a library and reading materials. An annexe at the back of the room, which also served as a cloakroom, was used for painting, although the child-level sink was at the opposite end of the classroom. She taught one area of the curriculum at a time. In the mornings, the children worked in ability groups on maths and language activities – mainly workcard or workbook based and linked to the maths and reading schemes – with occasional groups doing art activities with the non-teaching assistant. Children who had finished their 'basics' in the morning were expected to read. In the afternoon the children were allowed to sit in friendship groups to work on their topics.

Mrs C claimed that she felt that her practice already conformed to the LEA view of 'good practice'. After the course she had, however, 'made workbays' in her classroom.

> Soon after this, she had put her cupboards back against the wall because she didn't work an integrated day, and in any case the new arrangement had taken up too much space in a classroom that was already too small. However, the course had made her realize that it was better to keep the equipment and resources for each subject area together.
>
> (Alexander *et al*. 1989: 272)

She gave clear justifications for her style of organization and management of learning. She argued that the children in the catchment area of the school were difficult and needed the stability of a tightly structured day. She felt that the children would be confused if more than one curriculum area was being practised at a time, and besides she liked to monitor closely what everyone was doing. She also believed that children of 5 and 6 did maths and language best in the mornings when they were fresh.

In contrast Mrs D's classroom had areas set aside for language activities, a reading corner, a maths area which included a post-office/shop, and a home corner. Two tables served the function of space for 'overflow table-top work'; play activities such as sand and woodwork were outside the classroom. Her class of twenty-six vertically grouped 5–7-year-olds were allocated by age to three groups – reception, middle and top infants – and subdivided further for maths and language activities. Children worked in their groups simultaneously on maths, language or 'activities'. Her response to the LEA course had been that it had confirmed her belief in the value of mixed curriculum teaching and group work. After the course she had reorganized her classroom into curric- ulum-specific bays and concentrated on making resources more easily access- ible to the children. Although Mrs D believed that vertical grouping gave her the opportunity to concentrate on working intensively with groups, she admitted that the lion's share of her teaching time was directed at the younger children.

The effects of classroom layouts

It was clear that neither of these teachers had been encouraged to study the *effects* on children's learning of changing around furniture, re-siting resources or re-allocating floor space to different curriculum priorities. There was simply an *assumption* that such changes resulted in 'better' practice. Such assump- tions need to be substantiated by hard evidence. Teachers need support in the techniques of monitoring movement about a classroom, in the design and evaluation aspects of efficient siting and use of resources and floor-space. For example how can they justify space given to bulky equipment such as sand and water containers, which theoretically enhance children's learning of scientific and mathematical concepts, if observations such of those of Tizard *et al.* (1988: 58) indicate that sand and water are rarely used for teaching or learning?

In a sense Mrs C, although she did not conform to the model of 'good practice' defined by her LEA advisers, was responding with basic common sense to her ultimate rejection of 'workbays'. Her reasons, given her views on the most effective strategies for teaching in her classroom, were sound enough. Mrs D paid lip service to the value of practical activities and art work as the third aspect of curriculum priorities. But in fact it is significant that the sand and water and other practical activities were sited outside the classroom, where it is assumed any sustained interaction from her would be almost impossible. Whose response was the more honest – Mrs C's or Mrs D's?

One of the most positive findings of the Prindep evaluation has been the benefits of the LEA providing extra staffing in Leeds primary schools. This has allowed teachers to work together to try to resolve dilemmas in the manage- ment of learning. Leeds teachers agreed that one of the significant benefits of working collaboratively had been the opportunity to 'clarify instructional goals and decide on organizational procedures for achieving them' (Alexander *et al.* 1989: 229).

One of the major concerns of teachers is to encourage young children to concentrate on activities without 'flitting' from one unfinished task to another. There is evidence that children are distracted not by noise levels around them but by visual interference. In the Cleveland LEA nurseries described in the references to schemas in Chapter 2, teachers and nursery nurses have experimented with child-height screening to enclose work areas for sand, painting, construction, water, emergent writing, etc. Children are encouraged to concentrate on activities with perhaps one or two other pupils for extended periods of time. The screening ensures that the adults are able not only to observe these sustained learning episodes without distracting the children, but also to be aware when it is appropriate to intervene. An impressive feature of Montessori school classrooms is that children may pick up a small floor or table mat to ensure themselves some personal space to work out a play activity without fear of disruption. Some classrooms now provide screened-off, private areas for personal writing. This is a more sensitive strategy than to expect children to concentrate on a writing activity with the distraction of six or seven of their peer group writhing and chattering at a table around them.

Perhaps we also surround children with too much visual brilliance. There are schools which dazzle rather than provoke thought with their displays. The walls are dripping with extravagant and largely teacher-directed friezes. Mobiles swing wildly from every available ceiling space. One longs for the relief of a blank wall. The same sense of over-kill may characterize the vast range of resources available to children in some classrooms. The Montessori system offers children a controlled choice each day from a range of resources stored in baskets or containers on shelving. This adult structuring of activities may be helpful rather than restrictive to young children. Sometimes what is exhausting about supermarkets is the sheer enormity of the choice on offer! Perhaps some classrooms have the same effect on pupils.

The point is that the physical layout of a classroom should be based on systematic analyses of teaching and learning behaviours, rather than on blueprints of the visible features of so-called 'good practice'. But the Prindep team observed that little attention had been given in the Leeds LEA course on Classroom Organization to monitoring the effectiveness of teacher and pupil interactions:

> practice becomes talked about less in terms of operational detail than in terms of broad sentiments and commitments; less in terms of learning *processes* than in terms of what is called 'the environment of learning'; a kind of conceptual skirting around of the very act which is at the heart of education.
>
> (Alexander *et al.* 1989: 291)

We have already explored many of the critical issues related to classroom interactions in Chapter 3, but there are other issues to do with grouping arrangements, the organization of pupil and teacher time, curriculum differentiation and coverage which also need to be explored beneath 'the visible surface of practice' and it is to evidence of these aspects of classroom realities that we now turn.

The structuring of learning in the school day

Patterns of organization

The classroom organization of most teachers of 4–8-year-olds, in infant, first or primary schools, falls into one of three broad types.

1 The *skills and frills* approach – characterized by Mrs C's classroom – is basic skills in the morning, with children working as a class but on various levels of tasks in maths or language; and art, topic work, practical play activities or 'choosing time' in the afternoons.
2 The *rotation system* is when groups of children are moved around three basic curriculum areas – usually maths, language and 'activities' which include art and 'play' – during the day on a roundabout system.
3 In the *integrated day* children work throughout the school day, usually individually but sometimes in groups, at a variety of curriculum tasks at their own pace and level.

Within all patterns of organization, set class times for subjects like physical education and music or school television broadcasts will be dictated by access to timetabled hall space, television rooms/spaces, a piano and possibly a specialist musician teacher.

There is limited evidence from HMI surveys and research projects about the way in which infant teachers structure the school day. In the 1978 Primary Survey (DES 1978a) teachers were categorized as having two broad approaches: mainly didactic or mainly exploratory.

A didactic approach was one in which the teacher directed the children's work in accordance with relatively specific and predetermined intentions and where explanations usually, though not always, preceded the action taken by the children. An exploratory approach was one in which the broad objectives of the work were discussed with the children but where they were then put in a position of finding their own solutions to the problems posed and of making choices about the way in which the work should be tackled. The scope and timescale of the tasks involved were likely to be flexible and the path of the work was likely to be modified in the light of events; explanation by the teacher more often accompanied or followed action taken by the children.

(DES 1978a: 26, para 3.19)

Three-quarters of the teachers of 7-, 9- and 11-year-olds in the 542 primary schools surveyed employed a mainly didactic approach. Fewer than one in twenty adopted a mainly exploratory approach. One-fifth of the teachers were said by HMI to have 'employed an appropriate combination of the didactic and exploratory methods, varying their approach according to the nature of the task in hand'.

In the HMI survey of eighty first schools (DES 1982a) classroom organization and methods were defined as 'well suited to the children' in all the classes of sixteen of the schools. HMI went on to define what they meant by 'well suited':

In these schools there was a satisfactory balance between the opportunities provided for the children to find things out for themselves and more formal teaching. A good balance was kept between the activities initiated by the teacher and those chosen by the children. Individual, group and class teaching was arranged according to what was being taught and the needs of the children, rather than from a belief that one arrangement was superior to another.

(DES 1982a: 49, para 3.11)

In thirty-five of the schools such satisfactory methods were used in one or more of the classes, but in twenty-nine of the schools the children were either 'over directed' or 'given too little help in organising their work'.

In fact it is significant that in neither of the two HMI reports is much attention given to classroom organization and the management of learning. The terms used in the report are very vague, and there is little indication of the complex similarities and differences within and between classrooms in primary schools. Curriculum content on the other hand is given a great deal of attention in both reports.

In N. Bennett and Kell's (1989) study of 4-year-olds in classrooms, the infant teachers described their organization as 'integrated day', 'structured activities' and 'individualized learning'. These terms were used loosely, and the authors chose to give a flavour of the variations in patterns of organization by quoting directly from some of the teachers' accounts of their way of working:

An integrated day generally – a combination of class, group and individual work. I tend to put more emphasis on language, maths and science in the morning and craft work in the afternoon. The four year olds work to the same kind of pattern but their 'work' time tends to be for shorter periods and their free choice time tends to be more.

The children structure their own day, choosing activities out of those available. Certain work has to be done each day.

I have basically a thematic structure. I plan a term and then have weekly planning with built-in spontaneity.

An integrated day. I have a choosing board and the children select from the activities that are on offer – in tune with the nursery approach.

But these are simply descriptions of how the teachers in the study *claimed* that they organized their classrooms. There has been little systematic observation of the realities of infant classroom organization. The Oracle data on teacher and pupil types (Galton *et al.* 1980) is often generalized to infant practice on in-service courses or in reviews of educational research; but in fact all the Oracle data was drawn from observations in junior classrooms.

The project on *Extending Beginning Reading* (Southgate *et al.* 1981) provided some evidence of practice in the classrooms of 7-year-olds, though the data gathered focused on the teaching of reading. In Southgate's study the teachers devoted between twenty and one hundred minutes per day to listening to children reading. However, the child usually read to the teacher for only two- to three-minute periods, and this process was likely to be interrupted every thirty seconds. In teaching throughout the day the teachers switched their attention on average thirty-two times in each twenty-minute period of instruction. There was depressing evidence of 'the infant queue' where children would stand by the teacher's desk to read, or to have work marked, or to be given help when they were stuck or waiting to move on to a new activity. In some cases there would be dual queues, with one relatively fast-moving queue waiting for words to be written in wordbooks or for written work to be marked, while a second slower-moving queue of readers trailed through the task of reading aloud to the teacher as he or she frenetically marked and checked. If advisers and headteachers have conspired to spirit teachers' desks away in an attempt to dispose of 'the infant queue', the result has often been a perpetually moving queue with the teacher at its head, graphically described by Golby (1988) as 'a comet's tail of children with spelling books at the ready'.

Individualized learning

The data from Southgate's (1981) and Bennett's (1984; 1989) research point to the difficulties that teachers have in trying to implement a policy of individual-ized learning. In order to cover the basics, teachers frequently rely on mathematics and reading scheme workbooks, worksheets and workcards to keep young children 'busy' on individualized seat-based activities. The teacher's role then becomes reactive. Having briefly introduced a task to a child, or a group of children, his or her attention is often diverted to the learning or custodial needs of other children. The teacher is rarely able to observe the processes by which children complete the tasks assigned to them. The teacher may withdraw to sit at a desk, table or chair, and will interact with a child again, unless the child seeks help, only when the task is completed. It is difficult for the teacher to operate a diagnostic approach to checking and evaluating the finished work. In many cases the teacher will simply respond with a quick 'Yes, yes, yes', a string of ticks, with maybe a more searching response to any error the child has made. This pattern of feedback has the unfortunate consequence of children learning to expect teachers to comment only when they have done something wrong, but to give scant attention, other than a cursory 'well done', to their successful strategies.

When the Oracle team continued their research on managing children's learning in classrooms, they tried to elicit children's views of their expectations of teacher feedback. They presented some middle school children with a cartoon depicting a teacher marking a child's piece of written work at her desk and asked the children to write what the teacher was saying. The vast majority attributed negative comments to the teacher such as, 'Go and do it again,' or 'Pay attention' (reported in Galton 1989: 73). We appear to be inculcating children with an expectation of negative feedback from teachers.

It is clear from all the research studies quoted that the problems of trying to implement the Plowden doctrine of individualization are overwhelming for teachers of young children. Teachers are imbued with a sense of urgency to get the children literate, numerate and able to record. If they try to share their time out on an individual basis to a class of twenty-five to thirty-five infants, each child will have a very limited amount of direct teaching time. Consequently children have to operate independently on tasks for long periods of the day. When young children are engaged in practical activities, this can be a perfectly acceptable demand to make on them. But the problem is that children are required to 'work' on the basics as isolated individual learners, albeit seated alongside others of their peer group engaged on parallel tasks, without adult support. They are required to 'read' workcard instructions beyond their capability, or to record mathematical operations within mathematics work-book before their writing skills have developed. Consequently children spend much of their time 'coasting' in a fairly desultory way simply because they are overwhelmed, bored or frustrated by the tasks they have been assigned.

N. Bennett and Kell (1989) give some poignant examples of 4-year-olds in infant classrooms trying to respond to tasks beyond their capabilities. Mary was one such 4-year-old:

> The teacher's intention is sorting numbers by colour to provide experi-
> ence in writing numbers. The activity is drawn from SPMG *Infant
> Mathematics Stage 1*. The teacher's instructions were 'Now go and get
> your maths book' and 'do the next page.'
> 11.30 Mary has taken her workbox from the table and takes out *Infant
> Mathematics*, Heinemann Ed. Book Stage 1 . . . Sorting. Matching 1
> and 2 (SPMG) Page 10 – write 2. Mary has traced 2 – several times at
> the top of the page. Under this there are four sets of pictures (of,
> for example, 2 trees with a box alongside, where Mary should
> write 2).
> Mary has written a reversed 3 beside each set of two. Auxiliary
> walks over and asks what she has written. Mary does not reply.
> 11.38 *Auxiliary:* 'I'll go and get a rubber and rub them out.' She does so.
> Mary does another shape exactly as before, followed by another in

the next set below. Auxiliary counts the pictures with her. Mary counts correctly. Auxiliary draws 2. Mary draws. *Auxiliary:* 'Copy those again'. Rubs out Mary's 2s at the top of the page. Mary copies over the shapes. She starts from the bottom in each case. They end up looking fairly accurate. *Auxiliary:* 'Now do the sets where you got them wrong.' Mary goes back to the picture sets and does them wrong again. (She starts each number from the bottom as she did when tracing the numbers at the top of the page.) This time she rubs them out herself before Auxiliary sees them. Mary is nearly crying with frustration. She knows she has them wrong but just cannot get them right. Auxiliary re-appears from other side of table and tells her not to worry.

11.45   She tries again and gets one right and two wrong. Shrieks with frustration and hits Auxiliary on the arm to attract her attention. Gets two wrong again. Stands up and covers face with hands shouting 'Oh! Oh!'. Scribbles on second square where she should write 2. Auxiliary comes and sits next to her. She smiles sympathetically at Mary and says, 'I like that one', pointing to the only correct one.

Mary shouts to the teacher who happens to walk past the table, 'I can't do it. It keeps going wrong!' She has tears pouring down her cheeks. Teacher doesn't appear to really look at her. She says, 'Never mind. It doesn't matter as long as you try'. She ticks the work and tells Mary she can put her book away now.

(N. Bennett and Kell 1989: 68)

When the researcher questioned the pupil and teacher later about this activity, Mary was adamant that she could not do 2. 'I couldn't do it. It was too hard. I didn't like it. I don't like the books.' The teacher on the other hand rated the activity a success, arguing that the child got on with it, and it was a bit of her own work, and concluded 'She seems to like doing her maths book'. When asked what Mary would be doing next in the light of the day's work she replied, 'The next page'!

Other children are less conscientious when assigned tasks beyond their capability. Ray, for example, had been asked to make a Mother's Day card. He had been given a template, without any explanation as to what it said, with Mummy written on it. The researcher's observations were:

9.05   The teacher gives him the Mummy template and he starts to do this. Ray and Harry argue about what the template says: 'Daddy, Mummy . . .' Ray insists it says Daddy. They talk about Mummy and something to do with Readybreak. They start to tease another boy about his name, making up a new surname. Ray laughs. Starts colouring in again: 'We are working hard'. He moves the template and colours in the same letter as before, 'y' only, at the bottom of the

page. He carries on in the same way starting to write in the template.
It moves and he starts somewhere else. His paper has all
disconnected lines on it.

9.55 Ray and Harry creep away, bending double, but they come back
when the teacher moves. *Ray:* 'Harry, you want to go to the toilet,
shall we both go?' (He went just now.) The teacher comes and talks
to Harry. She writes his name. She looks at Ray's paper. *Teacher:*
'Haven't you done any shapes, Ray?' She goes and Ray gets another
shape – a diamond – and draws that more successfully once. He
does more colouring in. Using a pencil he draws in the 'y' in the
template. He takes the template, the wrong way up and draws in it,
then gets up, goes down the room, comes back, draws a bit. He
makes a few round shapes with tails on, then tries the template again
doing 'mmy' before moving it to the bottom of the page and doing
'my' again. Now he is working on the other side of the paper. He
stops to talk again. Meanwhile another boy takes the template and
starts doing it carefully. Ray wants the template back but is able to
find one on another table.

(N. Bennett and Kell 1989: 73)

In the pupil and teacher interviews after this activity, Ray could not explain
anything about Mother's Day and thought that the template was a pattern. The
teacher said that she was quite pleased with Ray's work.

These detailed observations of young children at work raise important
issues, first about the inability of teachers to gain accurate information about
pupils' learning unless they are able to observe the child on task, and second,
about the mismatch between children's capabilities and the tasks assigned to
them by teachers. In his detailed earlier study of the learning environment and
experiences provided by sixteen able (as defined by LEA advisory staff)
teachers of 6–7-year-olds, Bennett *et al.* (1984) claimed that more than half of
the language and mathematical tasks observed in the study were mismatched.

Overall there is a remarkably consistent picture for the two areas of the
curriculum. In number 43% of tasks were matched (40% in language),
28% were too difficult (29%) and 26% too easy (26%). In both areas of the
curriculum, high attainers were underestimated on 41% of the tasks
assigned to them, low attainers were overestimated on 44% of the tasks.
Middle groups got a diversified experience in number but tended to be
overestimated in language.

(N. Bennett *et al.* 1984: 45)

Bennett also raises important questions about the lack of clarity in teacher's
intentions for setting tasks (N. Bennett and Kell 1989). Sometimes the stated
intentions of the teachers were simply not reflected in the activity designated.
For example a child spent twenty minutes colouring in an extremely large
circle when the teacher's stated intention was shape recognition. Tracing

around a tree was the task set when the stated teacher intention was learning from left to right orientation.

Some tasks were set with multiple intentions, but rarely were children made directly aware of the *purposes* of any activity. In fact, the nightmare task of trying to give brief but clear instructions to a whole class of young children seated on a carpet, as often happens at the beginning of a working session, means that teachers habitually resort to focusing on procedural rather than cognitive issues as they set children off on activities. Bennett pin-pointed this discrepancy in his earlier study in 1984. In setting writing activities, for example, he noted that teachers would claim that their intention was to get children to write creatively, but invariably the final instructions to the children would emphasize correct spelling and neat handwriting. Children picked up these none too subtle messages when they were set writing tasks.

> They were clear about what would please their teachers. They recog-
> nised and were able to rate neatness as an important criterion and strove
> to finish another page to fulfil the quantity quota.
>
> (N. Bennett *et al.* 1984: 104)

Group work

If the individualization of learning is an illusory ideal, what about the altern-ative strategy of group work? Many infant teachers claim that they operate 'group work' in their classrooms; but what do they really mean? There are three common interpretations.

1 Six to eight children sit together around a table, working alongside each other, but essentially engaged in individualized tasks.
2 The teacher sits and concentrates on teaching one group of children at a time, throughout the day for sessions lasting between several minutes to, for example, the complete block of time between registration and playtime.
3 Children are encouraged to work collaboratively on shared activities.

In the first interpretation, a method of seating children can hardly be defined as group work in operational terms. Nevertheless, the criteria for grouping the children will almost certainly have an effect on the processes of learning. Teachers offer a variety of criteria for forming groups. The most obvious is ability, particularly in reading, but sometimes in mathematics. In Tizard's study of ILEA infant classrooms (Tizard *et al.* 1988) approximately half of the reception class teachers (of 5-year-olds) grouped children for teaching pur-poses, 55 per cent for maths and 48 per cent for language, mainly on the basis of the children's judged ability levels. Although 61 per cent of the top infant teachers (of 7-year-olds) used group teaching, their criteria included separat-ing children who did not work well together or accommodating friendship patterns. In Bennett's (1989) sample of seventy-one infant teachers about half used ability grouping, but one in four said they used mixed ability groups and one in six used friendship grouping. In mixed age classes they also grouped the children by age or date of intake.

We have already identified that teachers are aware of the dangers of self-fulfilling prophecies. Infant teachers often try to disguise the fact that children are grouped by ability in their classrooms. Groups will be given colour, animal, or flower labels – 'I want the chipmunks over in the maths area this morning with me, whilst the squirrels do art work with Mrs Brown, and the possums can get their Ginn workbooks out.' The animals are, of course, of a cuddly nature! Teachers have a range of euphemisms to describe their low ability groups to visitors: 'The ones that need a lot of support sit on Green table.' 'The slow children go out with the headteacher for extra reading in the mornings.' Children, however, are not so coy, and usually have a pretty shrewd idea of how they are ranked by teachers within the classroom.

Some children can stay within a grouping system, defined within weeks of school entry, throughout their primary schooling, particularly if the criterion used is reading test results. Patterns of dependency and dominance can build up amongst a small group of children who habitually work together. It is quite obvious in some cases that the absence of one dominant child from a table for a day will change the levels of work of the entire group, either for the better or worse. A dependent child who transfers at 11 to a secondary school system, where in many classes pupils are required to work in silence without peer group support or friendship, can be devastated by this abrupt change in working conditions.

Because of their anxieties about self-fulfilling prophecies many primary teachers prefer to use mixed ability grouping for teaching, but this can cause them all kinds of operational difficulties. Mixed ability teaching for ideological reasons may *not* prove to be an effective strategy for teaching purposes. Wendy, the teacher of 6–7-year-olds in the project referred to in Chapter 3 (Anning 1987), described the problems of pacing activities in a mixed ability group. In a task which involved children in putting names into alphabetical order, she had to slow down Shane, a child defined as of high ability, in order to accommodate the learning needs of the whole group:

> I said to the children, 'Now what comes first?' Shane actually came in straight away with the answer, but I didn't think it was wise at that point to say, 'OK, that's it'. I felt that. So I did actually ignore him and kept on saying it in the hope that I'd pick up the other children as well. My strategy to cope with that was to ignore Shane when he came through with the right answer quicker than I felt the other children latched on to it.

In another example, Jane, a reception class teacher in the project, admitted that she had seated 'a good reader' in a mixed ability group working on word recognition at a point on the table where the flashcards would be upside down for her (whereas they would be the right way up for the less able children) in order to stop the able child giving all the answers!

Wendy also worked with a mixed ability group on a task which involved introducing the concepts of machines and operators, using Bulmershe equipment. She had to intervene frequently to explain new ideas and procedures to the lower ability children. When she reviewed the tapes of the activities, she could see the contrast between the dynamics of this group learning situation and those of the matched ability group engaged on the graphical representation task (see pp. 50–2). She commented:

> If you have a group of children who are all one ability, I suppose the match of the task is better isn't it? So you start off talking; but then you can back off, because it's something you expect them to pick up on. Maybe this is a drawback of having a mixed ability group for this kind of task – I had to keep chipping in.

It is, I think, also significant that the exhilarating pace and progress in learning apparent in the graphical representation task, was the result of a *pair* of children of matched ability working together. Anybody who has suffered the frustration of being required to work on a shared task in small groups, perhaps six to eight, of fellow professionals at conferences or on in-service courses, will bear witness to the slow progress that is often made! Working in pairs is often more productive. It seems common sense that this should also be true of children's working preferences. Researchers have indicated how little collaborative work of any kind there is in primary classrooms (Tann 1981; Galton 1987; N. Bennett *et al.* 1984; N. Bennett and Kell 1989) and a contributory factor could be that children resist group work simply because the mechanics of working collaboratively can be so irksome. The middle school children whom Galton (1987) interviewed expressed some of this irritation. They rated the image of a group of children working together without the teacher present, but with a tape recorder strategically placed in the centre of the table, as their least popular classroom situation. The 8-year-olds gave such reasons as 'My friends make me silly', or 'There's no teacher' or 'You're worried if things go wrong'. The 12-year-olds interviewed were more positive about working with their peer group. They made such comment as 'It's good to work things out without the teacher' or 'You can have a laugh when you discuss', or more strongly, 'I would like to work with my friends and discuss things on our own because when you work with teachers they *always* stop you' and 'One could learn more from each other when there is no teacher to nag'.

This last comment draws attention to another important issue. Teachers do not really trust children to learn from their peer group despite the kind of evidence cited in Chapter 2 of the significance and value of children's learning from each other. The fact that a tape recorder was left in the centre of the table in the image presented to the children in Galton's study is not without significance. Children know that teachers feel the need to check on peer group learning. In Galton's study the children articulated very clearly their frustration at having the 'ownership' of peer group collaboration hijacked by the interference of the teacher. They told him that often, just as their group were beginning to find a way of tackling a shared activity, the teacher would join the group and suggest an alternative set of strategies. The teacher gives one set of messages through his or her instructions and another through subsequent sabotaging of the children's collaborative efforts. A child expressed his resentment:

> You feel a bit upset. You have put all that work into it and then the teacher suddenly changes it. You don't feel it is your piece of work. You feel as if it's the teachers. When you have done everything to it you think that's my piece of work and no-one else had done owt to it, but when the teacher's done something to it, it don't feel as good.
>
> (Galton 1987: 309)

On the other hand, the advantages of teachers working closely with a group in the role of *instructor* are clear because ironically it *does* then become possible for teachers to individualize learning. So, for example, Jane described the way in which she individualized a task within a small group activity for an immature learner, Brian. The task was to recognize the written form and sequence of the days of the week:

> 'T' in Tuesday has occurred before and I know these particular children will identify 'T' possibly with a character in the reading scheme which they've both used on colouring sheets. They've coloured this particular figure which is a little boy called Tommy. They've come across Tommy in one of the Trailer Books to the Link Up Scheme, and I do know that if I mention or show a picture of this boy Tommy, they will identify the letter 'T' more easily, 'T' for Tommy, and then they'll probably be able to transfer this learning to Tuesday and Thursday.
>
> I've drawn some sketches of things we do together as a class on different days to help them with the days of the week. I've included Brian's peg on one of them; I thought I'd do all this deliberately to see if he would notice his name. He can write his name – really very well – so I thought I'd see if he does notice it. The other clue was he had the tortoise on his peg, you see, and I thought well if he doesn't get his name, he'll get the tortoise – which he did. The only thing I'd done wrong was the colour of his towel!

Jane's close involvement with a group working on task meant that she could cue the children in to links with previous learning, as well as personalize the resources. In another activity, designed to encourage children to be more independent in their attempts to spell words, Janine, an above-average 5-year-old, was attempting to write the word 'kitchen'. Jane remembered that the child had recently drawn a witch for Halloween:

She was quick to recall another 'itch' word, because I said, 'What were you drawing round?', and I mentioned the two things specifically to see if she could recall the other one – and she did, so that made my job easier. . . . I had pointed out the 'itch' bit – I'd told her what it said – when she drew the witch the previous day.

Sometimes the teacher has to guide children towards appropriate links. In the 'machines and operators' activity, Wendy referred to several examples of children making associations between past and present learning. When she first introduced them to the word 'operator' she noticed that the children 'kind of shuddered' and put this down to the fact that it reminded the children of 'operations'. Ryan, a child who had arrived recently from Northern Ireland, was having great difficulties with mathematics *and* the Salford accents! Wendy commented:

> Ryan was unsure about the word 'operator'. He said, 'Do you mean like the apparatus in the hall?' and then, 'But do you mean it starts with "a" like Angela?', and although that had nothing to do with the task, at least it showed me that Ryan had learned other things that he didn't know a few months ago.

Another child tried to make sense of the task by comparing the word 'machine' and the emphasis on the thickness and thinness of logi-blocks to a real machine. 'Kevin said, "Ah, you mean like in a machine, it goes in thick and then gets squashed and comes out thin".' Wendy noticed that as Kevin was trying to make sense of this abstract process by comparing it to a real machine, he was actually working the ideas out with his hands – miming squashing and shaping shapes. Other children in the group repeated these machine-like actions when it came to their turn to change a logi-block by shape, size, colour or depth.

But occasionally inappropriate links are made. When the children were asked at one point to focus on the changes in the colour of the shapes, Suzy whispered into the teacher's ear, 'Is it like the song – Red and Yellow and Pink and Blue?' In this instance Wendy gently guided Suzy into a more appropriate strategy for selecting the next logi-block.

These examples illustrate a way in which individualized learning can be accommodated within small group instruction. The *task* is assigned by the teacher, but she encourages and supports a variety of *individual strategies* for pupils to adopt in tackling the task, and the teacher's responses are based on an intimate knowledge of the children's lives and learning experiences.

It is difficult to imagine how such close awareness of individual strategies and previous learning episodes might be used in class teaching; but there is evidence that class teaching can also be used effectively with young children despite the negative connotations of elementary school rote learning that the words conjure up.

Class teaching

During a recent five-week spell of working in Western Australia, I witnessed far more class teaching than I had seen in years of working in and visiting early years classrooms in the UK. Some of it was desperately bad – 6–7-year-olds being bombarded with information, followed by instructions to work from the blackboard at tasks which involved a lot of copying. But some of the teachers used class teaching, between sessions of group work related to the sessions, so effectively and with such panache, that the young children in their classrooms groaned when it was time to go out to play! I think there is some truth in Gage's (1985) belief that since class teaching is so deeply entrenched in teachers' repertoires of techniques, it would be more useful to find out how to improve class teaching than simply to send it underground when advisers or HMI were doing their rounds. Gage writes:

> Within the art form called classroom teaching there is also a great variation in quality. What I see as promising is research that accepts the basic parameters of classroom teaching: teacher-centeredness, whole-class organization, subject matter orientation, and much recitation interspersed with short lectures, discussions, tutoring and seat work. Such research will study the infinite variations possible within this stable art form, the variations that make the difference between superb, average and atrocious classroom teaching.
>
> (Gage 1985: 49)

Galton (1989) summarizes research on the effectiveness of direct instruction (see also Rosenshine 1987; Good and Brophy 1986). Of course, direct instruction can refer to work with an individual, a group or a class of pupils.

> These reviews stress the importance of structuring the learning experience – by proceeding in small steps at a rapid pace, and using frequent questioning – and of providing opportunities for overt, active practice, with plenty of feedback and corrections during the initial stages of learning new information.
>
> (Galton 1989: 105)

In the USA direct instruction has always been acceptable, but teachers in the UK baulk at some USA practices. For example, Bereiter and Engelmann's (1966) fierce methods of direct language instruction of disadvantaged young children (later developed in the 1970s into the DISTAR Learning Programme for pre-school children (Engelmann et al. 1972)) horrified many British teachers in the 1960s. In contrast, UK Early Years teachers habitually use whole class times for listening to stories, music, television or radio broadcasts or 'news times'. They may also claim that they use whole class discussions to stimulate language development. Systematic analyses of class 'discussions' (Willes 1983; Edwards and Westgate 1987) reveal only too clearly that the teacher dominates the talk in order to retain control over the class. A small percentage of children, often those that place themselves strategically in the main sight lines of the teacher, make brief contributions to the 'discussion'. The word discussion is simply not appropriate.

I feel that it is hard to justify the use of intense teacher questioning during whole class instruction. We only have to think of the memorable paragraph in Holt's (1984) *How Children Fail* when he reported asking children how they felt when he asked them a question. A child bravely responded, 'We gulp'. 'I asked them why they felt gulpish. They said they were afraid of failing, afraid of being kept back, afraid of being called stupid, afraid of feeling themselves stupid' (Holt 1984: 70). Feeling 'gulpish' within the confines of a small group activity can be difficult enough for children, as a sensitive teacher like Wendy acknowledges (see p. 53). Feeling 'gulpish' in a public arena such as class teaching time is something to which we should not perhaps subject young children.

But drawing young children together at various points of the school day, in what has been described as a 'wave' model (Chazan *et al.* 1987: 32), for short bursts of direct instruction may be appropriate for vocabulary extension, consolidating knowledge of letter sounds, practising simple mental arithmetic, introducing new information related to a class topic, demonstrating hand movements for letter formation – in fact, for a whole range of fairly routine activities.

The content of the curriculum

Since the control of the elementary school curriculum was relaxed in 1926 there had been a great deal of autonomy in the decisions primary school teachers made about curriculum content, although it was clear that the assumptions of parents, LEA officers and the government exerted pressure on schools to conform to expected patterns of provision. This autonomy ceased with the implementation of the prescribed content of a National Curriculum specified in the Education Reform Act 1988, which will be discussed in Chapter 5. However, it is important to look at pre-1988 practice, both the paper models and practical realities of curriculum provision in infant schools, since those practices are certain to influence the way the National Curriculum is taught at Key Stage 1.

Principles underpinning curriculum models

There are broadly three approaches to justifying the content of a curriculum offered in schools – as passing on 'desirable' knowledge, as servicing the needs of society, and as responding to the developmental needs of children.

Passing on knowledge

HMI identified six broad educational aims for primary and secondary schools in the government White Paper, *Better Schools* (DES 1985a). These aims, also recorded in the HMI document *The Curriculum from 5 to 16* (DES 1985b), are

1 to help pupils to develop lively, enquiring minds, the ability to question and argue rationally and to apply themselves to tasks, and physical skills
2 to help pupils to acquire knowledge and skills relevant to adult life and employment in a fast changing world
3 to help pupils to use language and number effectively
4 to instil respect for religious and moral values, and tolerance of other races, religions and ways of life
5 to help pupils to understand the world in which they live, and the interdependence of individuals, groups and nations
6 to help pupils to appreciate human achievements and aspirations.
                                                                  (DES 1985b: para 1)

HMI identified the following areas of learning and experience: linguistic and literary, mathematical, aesthetic and creative, physical, scientific, technological, moral and spiritual (DES 1985b: para 33).

These headings reflect a view that there are logically distinct forms of knowledge, each with its own distinctive but interlocking central concepts and specific methodology to which all pupils should have access (see Peters 1966; Hirst 1974). Despite the reluctance to accept the confines of what they regard as 'secondary school style subjects', primary practitioners have used the HMI framework in recent early years documents on curriculum planning. In the Inner London Education Authority document on *The Early Years: A Curriculum for Young Children* (ILEA 1987) the eight areas are further defined.

1 Linguistic and literary
   • about symbolic representation
   • about listening, talking, reading and writing
2 Mathematical
   • about recognizing and solving problems
   • about sorting and classifying, and identifying relationships and patterns
   • about pure numbers, measures, logic and sets, and their application to other areas
3 Aesthetic and creative
   • about symbolic representation, imaginative play, art and craft work, display, drama, movement and music
   • about doing their own and appreciating the creations of others
4 Physical
   • about body awareness, co-ordination and control
   • about spatial, manipulative and motor skills

- about imaginative use of the body
- about health and its maintenance

5 Scientific and technological
- about problem-solving
- about changing and controlling the environment
- about ourselves and living things
- about physical surroundings
- about forces, movement and energy

6 Moral
- about awareness of self and others
- about right and wrong, fairness and justice
- about being a member of a group and wider community

7 Spiritual
- about significance of life
- about sense of awe and wonder
- about myths and legends
- about religious experiences reflecting many faiths

8 Human and social
- about how we live and the world of work
- about relationships with each other and the environment
- about events and actions in the past and their relationship to the present and the future
- about physical and human conditions.

The ILEA authors emphasize the need to maintain a cross-curricular perspective in planning an early years curriculum, but they argue 'these separate subject strands usually remain undifferentiated, but they are none the less important in planning to ensure we provide breadth and balance in the curriculum' (ILEA 1987: 8).

Many infant teachers argue that 'knowledge does not fall into separate compartments' (CACE 1967: 187) and claim that they integrate all aspects of the curriculum in their teaching. In fact, the evidence from research into curriculum coverage in primary schools indicates that maths and English are taught as discrete areas of the curriculum, often using commercially produced schemes. Other aspects of the curriculum are often subsumed under the labels topic or project or theme-based work.

It seems clear that though children may not differentiate between 'subjects' in their learning, for teachers a framework such as that provided by the HMI aims, ensures that they plan a broadly based curriculum. In fact, 'integration' has not gone unchallenged as a panacea for primary curriculum and implementation. There was criticism in the 1978 Primary Survey (DES 1978a) that an integrated approach led to many children experiencing a disconnected series of learning opportunities which lacked rigour and cohesion. In the 1980s headteachers were encouraged to appoint curriculum 'consultants' amongst their staff to provide support throughout the school for aspects of the curriculum in order to ensure balance, cohesion and progression in planning. (Campbell 1985).

The needs of society

The second way of rationalizing curriculum content is that it should reflect the needs and demands of society; a social-imperatives approach. For example the emphasis on the world of work, consumerism and science and technology in the DES documentation of the Thatcherite years reflect an instrumental view of education as providing the state with 'value for money' by preparing pupils for the world of work. According to a social-imperatives view of the curriculum, education is seen as being controlled by powerful dominant groups who use the transmission of knowledge in schools to perpetuate privileges and hierarchies (Young 1971; Lawton 1980). The analyses of Sharp and Green (1975) and King (1978) identified these processes at work in infant classrooms, where the authors claimed that a middle-class, bourgeois culture was operating against the interests of working-class communities.

The needs of the child

The third approach is to take the nature, interests and patterns of development of the child as the basis for selecting the content of the curriculum. Blenkin and Kelly (1987) argue that a Developmental Curriculum takes 'common developmental principles' rather than 'common subject content' as the basis for planning the curriculum. 'The emphasis is placed on children's learning *through* experience or their growth in competence rather than on the learning of the knowledge and skills themselves' (Blenkin and Kelly 1987: 46). They argue that

> The developmental curriculum . . . emphasises feeling as well as logical thinking . . . and values a wide spectrum of symbolising activities, not just words and numbers. . . . It is important, therefore, that the opportunities we offer to children in the early years classroom are multi-sensory and allow for the representation of thought and experiences through such modes as the visual, auditory, tactile, graphic, linguistic, motor and logical-analytical.
>
> (Blenkin and Kelly 1987: 42)

W. A. L. Blyth (1984) has presented a case for an 'Enabling Curriculum' which is based on the concerns and interests of young children. He argues that 'In the course of planning the experiences that a school can contrive, it is easy to overlook those that are already present in children's lives' (W. A. L. Blyth 1984: 24). He rejects the over-used instructional objective/subject based model of curriculum planning. He argues instead for the content of the primary school curriculum to be based on six broad areas of experience which are central elements of children's lives and relate to their lives outside 'the school box':

1 growth, health and movement – because the growing child is faced with daily consequences of rapid changes in their physical development
2 communication – through the modes of speech, dance, music, drawing, model-making, etc.
3 interpretation of the world – through, for example, scientific understanding or the humanities
4 vision and imagination – through play, drama, storying, etc.
5 feeling, expression and imagination – through the arts, literature
6 values and attitudes – a planned sequence of moral and social education.

(W. A. L. Blyth 1984: 53)

Curriculum guidelines

Unifying the distinct strands of curriculum content, whatever the theoretical frameworks they use, is a daunting task for the primary teacher who is responsible for teaching the whole class the whole curriculum. The enormity of the task is set out in paragraph 12 of *The Curriculum from 5 to 16*:

> The curriculum should aim to be broad by bringing all pupils into contact with an agreed range of areas of learning and experience. It should also be balanced in that it allows the adequate development of each area. In addition, each major component should have breadth, balance and relevance and should incorporate a progression in the acquisition of knowledge and understanding. The various curricular areas should reinforce and complement one another so that the knowledge, concepts, skills and attitudes developed in one area may be put to use and provide insight in another, thus increasing the pupil's understanding, competence and confidence.

(DES 1985b: 7)

If we examine the paper versions of curriculum planning used in primary schools, there is evidence that the provision of school written guidelines to support teachers in this formidable task is variable. HMI (DES 1978a) found written guidelines for maths schemes in 85 per cent of the schools they surveyed, and 88 per cent had English schemes. In their survey of first schools (DES 1982a) HMI found that only 75 per cent had maths schemes and 78 per cent language schemes. Science, art, physical education and music guidelines were represented in between 36 and 44 per cent of schools in the two surveys, and drama in 18 per cent. In fact many teachers openly admit to 'doing their own thing' in interpreting school schemes of work even if they are provided. So faced with the task of selecting curriculum content, how do infant teachers plan?

Curriculum planning

McCutcheon (1980) studied the planning of twelve elementary teachers in Virginia using classroom observations, interviews with teachers, transcripts of meetings and analyses of the teachers' written plans. British teachers will instantly relate to the findings. Daily planning was written by teachers as an aid to memory; lists of activities that were crossed off, as with shopping lists, as they were completed. Most teachers agreed that they listed objectives only if required to do so by the principal (in the UK context substitute headteacher, adviser or school practice supervisor). One teacher wrote: 'Objectives are implicit in the activities. I know what the activity is for, but it doesn't make sense to write so much down.' The continuous processes of 'mental planning' were described by the twelve teachers as occurring any time, either during the school day or while walking down the aisles of supermarket stores. The teacher continued: 'The subconscious does a lot of sorting for you. You can think of many things almost simultaneously. The sorting is rapid, not logical or sequenced, and is different for different lessons.'

The teachers defined the purpose of this relentless process of reflective thinking (see Figure 2, p. 44) as to help lessons run smoothly or to anticipate and 'short-circuit' what might go wrong. In planning ahead, they referred back to previous experiences of teaching similar content and structuring similar activities – what worked and what did not. In other words, teachers are constantly rehearsing classroom routines in the same way that we as in-dividuals rehearse our personal encounters or daily work or travel routines as we clean our teeth in the mornings. The neat and tidy notion of the standard objectives model of planning: (1) specify objectives (2) select learning activi-ties (3) organize learning activities and (4) specify evaluation procedures (Tyler 1949) may be comforting for administrators and headteachers, but it does not match up to the way teachers prefer to plan. Nor does a tidy objectives model of planning take account of the contextual changes to which teachers must continually respond – an absent colleague means that you suddenly have six extra children to educate for the day; the community policeman calls; a wet playtime scuppers plans to set up art activities for the afternoon. As with rehearsals of the dramas we are anticipating in our personal lives, the scripts we plan for classrooms never quite turn out as we expect!

It also seems clear that teachers use curriculum content rather than aims and objectives as the basis for their planning. Many primary school teachers use the ubiquitous 'topic web'. They take a central concept like COLOUR or OURSELVES or a class visit to a castle, shopping centre or farm, etc. and map out related areas of interest or possible curriculum-based activities. For student teachers, inexperienced in the art of 'topic webs', this can result in some extraordinarily contrived links. But for experienced teachers the loose overall structure appears to provide a useful, if somewhat rough and ready, framework for their planning. What content-based planning does not allow for is a consideration of the skills and learning processes that children should be systematically acquiring.

If we go right back to the beginning and ask ourselves, 'What is worth teaching and learning for 4–8-year-olds?', we are likely to identify the *what* of the curriculum, including information, concepts and practical skills. These might be grouped under the HMI broad areas of learning and experience, as in the ILEA (1987) document, or in the current climate of a subject-based National Curriculum, under subject headings. But of equal importance is how children should be encouraged to develop attitudes such as curiosity, empathy, self-confidence and procedural skills such as problem-solving, observation, goal-setting, learning from mistakes – the *how* aspects of learning. If the 'what to learn' is represented alongside the 'how to learn' in a Venn Diagram (see Figure 4), in the intersection of the sectors we can represent what children actually do in classrooms. They experience, either through practical or reflective activities, make associations, hypothesize, reflect upon or represent in various ways the experiences they have. The learning processes identified in this intersection reflect the new insights into the way children learn discussed in Chapter 2. Through these processes children are continually restructuring their own particular understanding and knowledge. A model of planning such as this one which includes references to both curriculum content *and* processes, and at the same time recognizes how children learn in classrooms

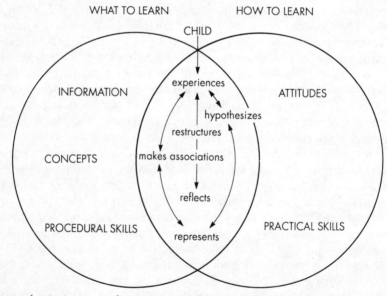

Figure 4   A content and process model for the infant curriculum

Source: Anning and Gates 1989: 26

Note: I am indebted to Judith Gates and colleagues from the advisory service and higher education who helped to design this model.

seems a more useful starting-point for planning than a list of 'aims and objectives,' and recognizes that all three approaches to justifying the content of the infant school curriculum – passing on knowledge, reflecting the needs of society and recognizing the learning needs of the child – are of equal importance.

The curriculum in practice

Finally, what happens when the paper planning of teachers is translated into learning activities in infant classrooms? We know that infant teachers expect

Table 1 The proportion of time children were observed in different activities (continuous observations of ninety 6–7-year-old children)

	Working time in class (%)	School day (%)
Working time in class		
Art/craft/construction, etc.	21	10
Writing	20	9
Maths	17	8
Oral language	23	10
Reading	4	2
Being allocated activities	4	2
Permitted 'free play'	3	1
Not assigned/wandering/other	4	2
Procedure (e.g. fetching books)	2	1
Uncodeable	2	1
Total	100	46
Other time		
Work activities		
Music/PE/rehearsals, etc.		4
Assembly		3
TV/tape recorders		1
Other school work, out of class		2
Total		11
Non-work activities		
Outside play/dinner-time		28
Lining up/tidying up, etc.		5
Toilet visits, etc.		4
Register/dinner money/milk, etc.		3
Uncodeable		3
Total		43

Source: Tizard *et al.* 1988: 51

and ensure that children spend up to two-thirds of the school day on maths and language activities (Bassey 1978; DES 1982a; N. Bennett *et al*. 1984; N. Bennett and Kell 1989; Tizard *et al*. 1988). The most recent and detailed analysis of the curriculum experienced by infant children is in the Tizard study (see Table 1).

Once we have recovered from the dismay at registering that 43 per cent of the children's day was spent in 'non-work' activities, we can turn to the 'work' categories. Overall the children spent 64 per cent of their time in 3R activities – 17 per cent of their working time in maths, 20 per cent in writing and 27 per cent in other language activities such as reading, discussion and story times. The team speculated that the surprisingly small amount of time designated to reading (4 per cent of class time) was a reflection of the emphasis placed in the schools on parents listening to children reading at home. In view of recent disquiet over a reported decline in reading standards of 7 year olds, leaked by educational psychology services in some LEAs (TES, 1990) this is worrying evidence. The three most common forms of writing were related to language workcards or workbooks, descriptive writing (describing a topic or picture) and story writing, though news and handwriting practice were also quite common. The great majority of maths tasks were in number – usually concentrating either on underlying number concepts, or on the formal operations of addition, subtraction, multiplication and division. Other areas of maths, with the exception of time, weight and length, were rarely observed, and no children were seen working on volume and capacity. (Many infant teachers simply find these too messy to set up and clear away.) Time spent on scientific activities was so minimal (e.g. activities such as tasting a variety of food for a topic on 'food'; testing water absorption for different materials) that they were recorded under 'Other school work' in Table 1.

Where was all the play that we are led to believe is so central to the infant school curriculum? Sand play occurred infrequently and water play was non-existent. Of the 195 constructional and creative activities observed, about half involved drawing, crayoning or tracing. Painting and claywork were only

Table 2   Free play activities observed in top infant classrooms

Free play activities	% of free play activities (N = 28)
Role-play (home/hospitals/shop)	46
Small figure play (doll/farm/ fort/cars, etc.)	21
Sand play	14
Board games	11
Uncodeable	7

Source: Tizard *et al*. 1988: 58

relatively infrequently seen. 'Free' play was extremely rare, accounting for 1 per cent of the school day. A breakdown of the twenty-eight free play activities observed shows that most were imaginative role-play or doll play of one form or another. The breakdown is given in Table 2.

These then are the kinds of curriculum realities that faced infant-aged children in their classrooms in the 1980s. Will the implementation of a National Curriculum drastically alter these patterns in the 1990s? It is to this issue that we turn in Chapter 5.

5

A National Curriculum for 4–8-year-olds

On 29 July 1988 the Education Reform Act became law. The Act legislated for far-reaching changes in the educational system in England and Wales. The powers of LEAs were drastically curtailed. Parents were given the right to choose the schools their children should go to – providing the school had the capacity to accommodate them. Under the terms of Local Financial Management, control of the budgets of schools with more than 200 pupils was devolved to the governors. The Act also provided for the governors of schools with more than 300 pupils to apply, with the consent of a majority of parents, through a secret ballot, to 'opt out' of the LEA system and into direct DES funding. It is difficult to foresee the exact consequences of these radical administrative and financial changes for infant and first schools. Though few have more than 200 pupils, some LEAs have already decided to apply Local Financial Management arrangements to small schools.

The more immediate concerns of infant schools have been with the introduction, under the terms of the Act, of a National Curriculum, overseen by the newly established National Curriculum Council (NCC) and the Curriculum Council for Wales (through the Welsh Office, WO). The Secretary of State is empowered to 'make orders', on the advice of the NCC, concerning programmes of study and attainment targets on the prescribed subjects defined as constituting a National Curriculum 5 to 16 for Key Stages 1 to 4: for ages 5–7, 7–11, 11–14, 14–16.

There is an unequivocal statement in Sub-clause 1(2) of the Act that a National Curriculum should be 'balanced and broadly based' and should:

(a) promote the spiritual, moral, cultural, mental and physical development of pupils at the school and of society; and

(b) prepare such pupils for the opportunities, responsibilities and experiences of adult life.

In their anxiety about the prescribed core and foundation subjects, teachers tend to lose sight of this overriding sub-clause.

The prescribed National Curriculum subjects are:

1 *Core subjects* English, Mathematics, Science, Welsh (at Welsh-speaking schools)
2 *Foundation subjects* History, Geography, Art, Music, Technology, Physical Education, and a Modern Foreign Language (the last not at Key Stages 1 and 2)
3 *Religious Education* Under the terms of the new Act, religious education will be taught according to locally defined Agreed Syllabuses, which will be reviewed by Standing Advisory Councils on RE (SACRES).

There is a clear statement in the document circulated to all teachers in maintained schools, *National Curriculum: From Policy to Practice*, that the 'new requirements' are to be embodied in 'the good classroom practice which is the key to successful implementation of the National Curriculum' (DES 1989a: 11.2). As the programmes of study drawn up by the subject-based Working Groups have been delivered to schools, teachers have been reassured that the proposals made are broadly in line with what is currently defined as 'good practice'.

The Working Groups for the core subjects were required to produce programmes of study at great speed. During the short periods of consultation on the Interim Reports, some content related to Levels 1 to 3, the levels it is assumed will be covered by Key Stage 1, has been refined. It is not surprising that there were some refinements to be made. A quick run through the identities of the Working Groups will indicate very few members with experience of teaching at primary level and even fewer with experience of working with 5–7-year-old children. Despite the fact that the National Curriculum was introduced to 5-year-olds first, the secondary ethos of 'subject' expertise appears to have provided the main criteria for deciding the composition of the working groups. We are still struggling to get the expertise of early years educators recognized within the profession.

A national system of assessment will be the responsibility of a second body, the Schools Examination and Assessment Council (SEAC). Members are appointed by the Secretary of State to design and implement standard assessment tasks (SATs) for children at the end of the four designated Key Stages – at 7, 11, 14 and 16. The cohort of 5-year-olds first introduced to the core subjects in September 1989 were the guinea-pigs for a pilot run of the first Standard Assessment Tasks (SATs) of the National Curriculum in 1991. We shall return to the vexed question of assessment in Chapter 6.

Table 3   Timetable for introducing core and foundation subjects

| | | | Key Stage | | | |
			1	2	3	4
Mathematics and science	Introduction First reported	Autumn	1989	1990	1989	1992
	assessment	Summer	1992	1995	1993	1994
English	Introduction First reported	Autumn	1989	1990	1990	1992
	assessment	Summer	1992	1995	1994	1994
Technology	Introduction First reported	Autumn	1990	1990	1990	1993
	assessment	Summer	1993	1995	1994	1995
History and geography (provisional)	Introduction First reported	Autumn	1991	1991	1991	1994
	assessment	Summer	1994	1996	1995	1996
Art, music, PE, modern languages (provisional)	Introduction First reported	Autumn	1992	1992	1992	1995
	assessment	Summer	1995	1997	1996	1997
Welsh	Introduction First reported	Autumn	1990	1990	1990	1992
	assessment	Summer	1993	1995	1994	1994

A timetable for the proposed introduction of the core and foundation subjects and assessment procedures is set out in Table 3.

Suddenly in September 1989, the spotlight was turned on to infant schools. As the National Curriculum was introduced to 5-year-olds in the first instance, the first stages had to be seen to be successful. Parents had to be convinced of the need for a centralized system of curriculum control with a related programme of national testing. There was a flurry of official reports on the early years of schooling. A Select Committee on Achievement in Primary Schools reported in July 1986. A second Select Committee reported on the Under Fives in 1989 and a further report chaired by Angela Rumbold on the quality of educational provision for children under 5 followed.

How are the teachers in infant and first schools coping with the changes imposed by the Education Reform Act? In this chapter we shall examine evidence of their initial reactions and discuss some of the implications of the policy changes for the curriculum for 4–8-year-olds in the 1990s.

A National Curriculum for infant and first schools

Many primary teachers reacted angrily to the concept of losing their traditional autonomy in the choice of the content of the curriculum they were offering their classes. There was hostility to the notion of a subject-based curriculum framework. Primary teachers argued that teachers in primary schools worked in an integrated way, not in subject areas; that young children did not see knowledge in separate subject compartments; and that their planning was based on themes, topics or projects rooted in the children's interests and immediate experiences.

As we have seen from the evidence presented in Chapter 4, in reality the 'basics' of language and maths *have* been taught as discrete areas of the curriculum. The third 'basic', science, hardly figured in the infant curriculum, other than as 'nature study' until the 1980s. The rest of the curriculum – history, geography, moral and religious education – has been planned around the 'topic web'. Art often became the servicing agent for a project, with learning experiences, media, and techniques introduced simply because of the require-ments of wall displays or project folders. In general, the content of physical education and music curriculum was as self-contained as the maths and language curricula, though perhaps dance or movement sessions or the choice of new songs to be learned might be loosely linked to the current topic – 'The Wheels on the Bus' for a project on Transport; 'squirrels hiding nuts' dances for a project on Autumn . . .

The claim that children's interests dominate the curriculum of infant schools may also be challenged. Many excellent infant teachers do initiate visits and introduce lively starting-points to stimulate young children's learning. Their overall planning is based on a genuine responsiveness to the kinds of things their class of children find interesting. But many of their colleagues have annually made assumptions that every new class of children they meet *will* be interested in Bread; Spring lambs, bunnies, catkins and tadpoles; and The Seaside, and always in that order! In fact, many children in the 1990s are deeply interested in all aspects of television (particularly the soap operas such as *Neighbours* and *EastEnders* and cartoons), clothes, football, pop music and dance, bikes, technical toys (often based on comic, film or television char-acters), shopping, how things around the house work, why natural phenomena occur. How many of these kinds of children's interests are routinely reflected in infant teachers' choices of topics? In an honest child-centred curriculum, perhaps they should be.

But education is a deeply conservative process. Jean Rudduck expresses the dilemma well.

The inertia of past meanings is a formidable barrier to change. In education, you cannot create a vacuum in which to grow a new set of meanings and practices; you cannot stop teaching for a year in order to work together in a different way. The show must go on. It is against such pressures that the task of change has to be undertaken.

(Rudduck 1986)

Infant teachers, after initial angry reaction to the proposals for a National Curriculum based on subject labels, simply knuckled down to making the best compromises they could between their preferred ways of designing and implementing the curriculum and the requirements of the Programmes of Study specified by law. In fact, their protestations about a commitment to an integrated approach to curriculum planning forced many school staffs to become more rigorous in their long-term planning of themes and topics than they had ever been before. In a sense their bluff had been called. Moreover, the issues of overlap and progression in curriculum content, identified by HMI as a problem as long ago as the 1978 Survey (DES 1978a), were addressed perhaps for the first time in many primary staffrooms in the months leading up to September 1989 as teachers struggled to come to terms with the Programmes of Study and Attainment Targets for Science, Mathematics and English – the only subject documents then available to them – without losing sight of their topic based approach to planning.

The core subjects

English

There has been a great deal of research and in-service training in the teaching of language in primary schools. It is probably the one aspect of schooling with which most primary teachers feel confident. The Working Party was able to draw on these strengths in compiling the programmes of study for Key Stage 1 for what is called English, though most primary practitioners would feel more comfortable with the label Language. In the final orders, after pressure had been exerted by practitioners, equal weighting was given to the three profile components – Speaking and Listening (AT1), Reading (AT2) and Writing (ATs 3–5). It was thus acknowledged that the best approach to teaching language is a holistic one.

Speaking and listening

In Chapter 2 the work of Tizard and Hughes (1984) and Wells (1987) was discussed. They stressed the importance of building on children's competencies in their home language by setting up opportunities in schools for genuine conversations about shared experiences. In the introduction to the programme of study for speaking and listening, the importance of encouraging children to 'encounter a range of situations, audiences and activities which are designed to develop their competence, precision and confidence in speaking and listening, irrespective of their initial competence or home language' is stressed (NCC/WO 1989a: 13). It is significant that though earlier drafts of the programmes of study made references to bilingualism in primary classrooms, these were deleted from the final version of the Orders. In the Non Statutory Orders attention is drawn to 'how bilingual speakers from the community or support services might assist children, through the use of the home language, to a better command of English'. This recommendation has particular resource implications for school starters whose home language is not English. Funding the provision for bi-lingual support will be complicated by the requirements of governing bodies under Local Management of Schools arrangements to control school staffing budgets.

Throughout the document, the emphasis is on learning through language as discourse between peers and adults, rather than on language taught by the teacher as expert. However, speaking and listening activities should be planned, not simply left to chance, and should include access to stories and poems from different cultures, responding to audio and visual recordings, discussion and collaborative work, talking about shared class and home experiences, play and drama, giving and receiving simple explanations, in-formation and instructions and asking and answering questions. It is made clear that pupils unable to communicate by speech may use technology, signing, symbols or lip-reading to speak and listen.

Reading
The approach to the teaching of reading stresses that reading activities should

> build on the oral language and experiences which pupils bring from home. Teaching should cover a range of rich and stimulating texts, both fiction and non-fiction, and should ensure that pupils regularly hear stories, told or read aloud, and hear and share poetry read by the teacher and each other.
>
> (NCC/WO 1989a: 15)

The Orders thus stress two important features of what is currently recognized as good practice in the teaching of reading.

First, good practice builds on what children bring to the learning situation rather than disempowering them by presenting tasks that are divorced from their 'realities'. The work of Frank Smith (1971; 1978) in Canada, Marie Clay (1979) in New Zealand, and Jessie Reid and Margaret Donaldson (1979) in the UK, emphasized the importance of facilitating children's access to reading by providing texts which recognized the common patterns of language use and vocabulary familiar to young children and by encouraging them to use their own writing as a source of reading. The innovative *Breakthrough to Literacy* (Mackay *et al.* 1970) materials encouraged this approach. In the UK Reid and Donaldson argued that children should also be encouraged to make sense of the functional language all around them – advertisements, labels, street signs, posters – in their homes and in the streets.

The second and more controversial feature of current good practice is that 'real' story and picture books are advocated as the best diet to encourage children to gain and acquire independent reading habits (J. Bennett 1979; Waterland 1985). The teacher or parent is encouraged to offer a model of reading behaviour to the child. The approach is called 'the apprenticeship model' of teaching reading. The artificial, stilted texts and formalized conventions of the kind of reading schemes in common use in the 1960s and 1970s have been discredited. It was argued that graded reading schemes offered children 'meaningless' reading tasks which they simply completed to 'please teacher'. Instead children were to be encouraged to approach reading as an active, interesting and above all purposeful activity. The publishers quickly responded by producing reading schemes which looked like real books! Reading schemes are not mentioned in the programmes of study, despite the fact that many schools still use them as the basis of their teaching of reading, and many parents still wait anxiously to see which coloured book within the graded scheme system their children will emerge clutching at the end of the school day.

Reference is made in the programme of study to the need to guide children to use 'the available cues, such as pictures, context, phonic cues, word shapes and meaning of a passage to decipher new words' (NCC/WO 1989a: 16). The subskills of reading, which in the past were habitually taught as isolated drills using flashcards, lists of words or phonics, are to be taught in the context of real reading activities. Children should also be encouraged 'to develop the habit of silent reading'. Emphasis is also given to reading for information – and the implication is that study skills should be taught to children from the earliest stages of learning to read. Non-sighted children will have alternative methods such as braille to demonstrate their capabilities; those that are unable to read aloud may use signing.

Writing

There has been far less research on the early stages of writing in schools, though both F. Smith (1982) and Clay (1975) moved on to study the development of writing skills, and in this country Andrew Wilkinson (1986), Helen Cowie (1984) and Nigel Hall (1987) have contributed to a growing understanding of how young children develop competence in writing.

The programme of study for writing includes three subdivisions – writing, spelling and handwriting. This approach sits uneasily alongside the holistic approaches to speaking/listening, and reading for pleasure/functional purposes. One suspects that the divisions have been included as a sop to the demands for better standards of spelling and handwriting in our schools. Explicit references to teaching an understanding of grammatical terms and the conventions of fullstops and capital letters, albeit in the context of discussion about children's own writing, are included, but the Orders put a surprisingly enlightened emphasis on teaching children to understand how language works, rather than on teaching the formal conventions of grammar.

The general approach to teaching writing continues the theme of building on what children already know about print and encouraging them experiment with communicating through 'emergent' writing (see Hall 1987) as well as through drawing and diagrams. As with the apprenticeship model of teaching reading, children should also be offered models of the writing process. They should then be encouraged to write both individually and in groups 'in different contexts and for a variety of purposes and audiences'. Children with special educational needs should be encouraged to use technological aids wherever possible to enable them to complete programmes of study, and those whose disability makes handwriting impossible will be exempt from the handwriting aspects of the programme of study.

It could be argued that far from discouraging teachers from using 'progressive' approaches to language teaching at Key Stage 1, the English programmes of study have given them a full licence to operate. Many teachers may in fact be jolted into adopting practices that have been seen up to now as rather avant garde.

Mathematics

In the NCC Non-Statutory Guidance for Mathematics, mathematics is defined as 'a way of viewing and making sense of the world. It is used to analyse and communicate information and ideas and to tackle a range of practical tasks and real-life problems' (NCC/WO 1989b: 2.1, A2). The creative aspect of mathematics is emphasized. 'Mathematics also provides the material and means for creating new imaginative worlds to explore. Through exploration within mathematics itself, new mathematics is created and current ideas are modified and extended' (NCC/WO 1989b: 2.2). This broad approach reflects the view of mathematics taken in the Cockcroft Report (DES 1982b) that children 'need to learn to think with mathematics rather than merely respond to routines'.

The programmes of study are set out under five broad headings: number, algebra, measurement, shape and space, and handling data. There are fourteen attainment targets altogether. Attainment targets 2 to 8 and 10 to 14 relate to the knowledge, skills and understanding pupils need to acquire. Attainment Target 7, 'Using graphical representation of algebraic functions', does not apply to Key Stage 1. Attainment targets 1 and 9 relate to using and applying this knowledge, skills and understanding – using mathematics, communicating in mathematics and developing ideas of argument and proof – and underpin all the other aspects of the programmes of study. It is made clear that the programmes of study do not specify 'a mathematics curriculum in action'. They are to be seen as 'the common framework within which all schools must construct their own policies and plans for mathematics'.

In the Non-Statutory Guidance it is pointed out that learning in mathematics is not a tidy and linear process but rather progression 'is to do with the way in which teachers and pupils explore, make sense of and construct pathways through a network of ideas'. Each child's progression through the network will be different, depending upon what previous knowledge and experience he or she brings to new learning experiences. The role of the teacher is

> to organise and provide the sorts of experiences which enable pupils to construct and develop their own understanding of mathematics, rather than simply to communicate the ways in which they themselves understand the subject.

> (NCC/WO 1989b: C2)

Current practice in infant school mathematics
How will the proposed common framework match up to the current mathematical experiences offered to children in infant schools? Evidence offered by HMI in the survey of first schools (DES 1982a) was that only one-fifth of the eighty schools surveyed achieved 'a good balance between learning how to perform a calculation and using it in a practical setting'. In many of the schools there was an over-emphasis on computation 'to such an extent that children lacked opportunities to apply mathematical ideas to everyday experiences and sometimes failed to understand the calculations they undertook' (DES 1982a: 20–1).

The NCC prescriptions sound very fine, but the realities for teachers of trying to teach through practical activities, and to base their interventions on a close understanding of the particular pathways to understanding each child may take, are complex and demanding. Extracts from teaching and learning episodes such as Wendy working on mathematical tasks (see Chapter 3) demonstrate that skilful teachers can and do cope with such complexities.

But the temptation to which many teachers succumb is to rely on a maths scheme to keep children 'occupied', with each child working individually at their own pace (see N. Bennett *et al.* 1984; Tizard *et al.* 1988). At the end of a session, there is then some recorded evidence of the children having 'done some maths'. In a practical activity the evidence of learning often 'disappears' at the end of the session into a pile of plastic in a storage box. A teacher must be confident enough to live with such ephemeral outcomes. And of course children must be persuaded that there is maths outside a workbook. Maths workbooks are generally popular with children because on the whole the tasks set allow them to coast – or copy from a friend – and, like all learners, they will settle for an easy ride if the opportunity is offered!

Children's strategies in mathematical learning
The NCC document suggests that children should be encouraged to use a variety of strategies in tackling mathematical tasks. 'Working in the head' should be encouraged, as well as pencil and paper and the use of calculators and computers to find solutions. In their study of mathematics in first schools,

Desforges and Cockburn (1987) point out that within a group of children each may opt for a different route through a mathematical task set by the teacher. They might recall a similar task done recently and simply repeat a formula that appeared to be successful. They might even turn back to check earlier solutions in their workbooks. They might pick up on a solution offered by someone else in the group, or at worst simply copy the answers from a neighbour. They may memorize instructions given by the teacher at the start of the exercise, or simply 'read' the teacher's prompts as they are working through an activity. They may also decide to use an easier method than that suggested by the teacher, often adapting their behaviours or doctoring recorded work before it is checked so that they appear to have used the 'correct' procedures.

Sometimes children invent remarkable strategies of their own. Hughes (1986) gives an irresistible example of 'an interesting finger counting strategy' from his observation of 6-year-old Mark at work:

> He responded to the written problem '5 + 6 = ' by laying one hand flat on the table, and saying, 'Five'. He then laid a pencil down next to his hand. He put his other hand down on the other side of the pencil, and said, 'Six'. Finally, he added up all eleven items (ten fingers and pencil), using his nose to count with! It was an extremely impressive performance.
>
> (Hughes 1986: 133)

In National Curriculum terms, the teacher's role is to keep account of each child's progression through the levels of attainment in each of the five broad areas of mathematical learning – number, algebra, measurement, shape and space and handling data – both at a formal recorded level, but also in constantly updating their awareness of what the child can do as they observe children on tasks.

Children's understanding of mathematical symbols
An area not tackled in the NCC documentation is children's understanding of mathematical symbols. Martin Hughes was one of the researchers working with Margaret Donaldson on the reinterpretation of children's responses to Piagetian tasks in the 1970s (see pp. 22–4). He pursued the idea expressed by Donaldson that children 'must become capable of manipulating symbols' (Donaldson 1978: 88–9), and that the role of the adult is to extend children's understanding of the power of symbol systems. Hughes' (1986) work parallels research into children's emergent writing in the UK.

He carried out a series of experiments with nursery and infant school children to explore both their ability to handle and represent the conventions of number symbols, and their ability to understand and use the far more abstract processes represented by mathematical signs such as plus and minus. He discovered that young children used a range of strategies when they were asked to represent a number of bricks on paper. At pre-school level 4-year-olds tended to use arbitrary and idiosyncratic responses – scribbles or 'letters' to represent the bricks. By 5, children were more likely to make pictographic responses; that is drawing the number and position of the bricks almost as they saw them on the table, and in some cases actually drawing around the bricks physically. At 6 or 7, children used either iconic responses – simple tally systems, circles or other objects were drawn to indicate the number of bricks. Finally children used symbolic responses – writing the numerals or the number words 'one', 'two', 'three', etc.

When Hughes went on to ask children to represent mathematical processes of addition and subtraction by taking from or adding bricks to those on the table, he was astonished to discover that no child in a sample of ninety-six 7-year-olds used the symbols + or − in their representations. And yet (as Margaret Donaldson pointed out in the foreword to his book) 'three-quarters of these children were regularly using these symbols when doing addition and subtraction sums in school'. Hughes concluded that we need to be far more explicit in teaching children about the use and application of mathematical symbols. He devised a series of games using magnetic numbers and mathematical symbols attached to tins of objects to demonstrate mathematical operations. He argued that teachers should explicitly teach 'the formal code of arithmetic', and set up learning situations where children see the point of using the code to solve a problem or accomplish something which has a purpose for them. Such a purpose might be, for example, keeping account of the number of bottles of milk to be cancelled for absentees; or buying the ingredients within a set weekly budget for a baking activity and handling the additions and subtractions needed. The argument then is 'not to avoid mathematical symbols in a child's earlier experience. Rather one should capitalise on situations where children feel a need for symbols' (Buxton 1982, quoted by Hughes 1986: 178).

Finally it is important that teachers introduce children to the language of mathematics and model the use of technical vocabulary, as Wendy did when she introduced the new concepts of 'machines' and 'operators' (see p. 86). We cannot assume that young children understand what we mean by words like 'number', 'a set of', 'add', any more than they know what we mean by 'letter', 'sentence' or 'write'. Explicit explanations must be given.

Sometimes young children will buck the system, defying the 'logic' of adult strategies and explanations, as Mark did with his ingenious counting procedure. In the project involving six primary teachers at work (Anning 1987), 4-year-old Paul had been encouraged by his nursery teacher to sort Kugeli balls into sets by colour. He was rapidly tiring of the routine and becoming bored with the repetition of colour names and 'the same as' or 'not the same as'. He placed a black Kugeli ball amongst a carefully sorted set of yellow balls and stared defiantly at the teacher. 'Why have you put that black one with the yellow set?', she asked. 'Because he's the boss', replied Paul very firmly and stalked off.

Science

In their 1978 survey of primary schools, HMI reported critically on the state of science teaching:

> Few primary schools visited in the course of this survey had effective programmes for the teaching of science. There was a lack of appropriate equipment; insufficient attention was given to ensuring proper coverage of key scientific notions; the teaching of processes and skills such as observing, the formulating of hypotheses, experimenting and recording was often superficial. The work is observational and experimental science was less well matched to children's capabilities than work in any other area of the curriculum.
>
> (DES 1978a: 5.66)

HMI also reported that what little science was taught tended to be in biology rather than the physical sciences, and that one of the greatest obstacles to improving the quality of primary science teaching was 'that many existing teachers lack a working knowledge of elementary science appropriate to children of this age' (DES 1978a: 5.83).

Various initiatives were launched in the 1980s to improve the quality of science teaching in primary schools. The dissemination phase of the Progress in Learning Project (Harlen *et al.* 1977a and b) concentrated on alerting teachers to the need to work closely with children, to observe the processes by which they acquired scientific skills and concepts, and to match learning experiences to their observed capabilities. The Assessment of Performance Unit, which was set up from 1974 to monitor children's learning in schools, began to deliver some fascinating information about the difficulty many 11-year-olds had in science-specific skills. The implication was that primary teachers needed to address related issues about the teaching of such skills (APU 1984). Many LEAs took advantage of the DES funding offered under the Educational Support Grants (DES 1984) and appointed advisory teachers in science to work alongside class teachers. Schools appointed Science Co-ordinators and sent them off on in-service courses to gain some confidence in tackling a coherent school policy in science. The publishers began to produce science schemes for primary schools. In 1985 DES published a policy statement on the teaching of science – *Science 5–16: A Statement of Policy* (DES 1985c). By 1989 HMI reported considerable improvements in primary science teaching (DES 1989b) but science remains an uncharted area of the curriculum in many infant classrooms.

The programmes of study in science

In the National Curriculum Science document (NCC/WO 1989c) there are two profile components: Exploration of Science and Knowledge and Understanding. Within Exploration of Science there is only one attainment target at ten levels. It is concerned with children's 'abilities to communicate, to relate science to everyday life and to explore'. As in the process profile component of the maths programme of study, the Exploration of Science is designed to underpin the children's acquisition of knowledge and understanding in science. The Knowledge and Understanding Profile Component contains sixteen sets of attainment targets – of which thirteen apply to Key Stages 1 and 2 – such as The Processes of Life, Genetics and Evolution, Earth and Atmosphere, Forces, Energy. Although teachers are reassured that the starting-point for scientific learning will be 'set within the everyday experiences of children', there seems to be an enormous amount of content to cover in the primary years. Teachers are also being encouraged to do a great deal of practical 'explorations and investigations' in their classrooms.

The NCC science prescriptions create difficulties for infant teachers. First, they have little experience of setting up and monitoring 'explorations and investigations'. Second, the lack of scientific knowledge amongst a pre-dominantly female, arts-based teaching work-force, identified as a source of difficulty as long ago as 1978 by HMI, and restated within a 1989 report by HMI on the teaching of science in primary schools creates genuine and understand-able anxiety. It is a fine idea to set up open-ended learning situations which will encourage children to ask questions. But what do you say to the child who asks, 'Why do aeroplanes stay up in the sky?' or 'Do ants have hearts?', when you really have no idea at all what the answer might be? Of course, you should then quickly dispatch the child to reference books to find the answers; but reference book explanations are often at a reading level way above the young child's capability. Moreover, 'scientific' explanations of complex phenomena, often intellectually demanding for adults, can be distorted by attempts to explain them at a very simple level. Both the child and the teacher can remain baffled rather than enlightened.

Ros Driver (1983) has been extending her project on Children's Learning in Science to infant classrooms. The project takes a 'constructivist' view of children's learning in science. Driver argues that children of all ages bring to school science activities a diversity of ideas and explanations about natural phenomena and the world around them. For example when forty 5-year-olds were asked what they knew about air, most replied that 'air is everywhere'; a few had other ideas such as that air was also in water (because fish need to breathe) or that it came from the clouds or the sky. Driver maintains that it is essential that teachers begin to build up an understanding of what children's conceptual maps of scientific phenomena might look like. We have been offered the 'certainties' of a Programme of Study for Key Stage 1 in science on the basis of very little evidence of how young children's learning in science progresses.

John Stannard (1988) gave an example of a young child trying to build upon previous learning experiences in science – this time from a school-initiated situation.

'Kevin is 6.5 years old. He has been out with his class to explore the effects of echoes in a large pedestrian subway near the school, as part of a science topic about sound. He was very interested in how sound travelled and the explanations about soundwaves which his teacher had given. Some days later he came to her and said, 'I can tell you how people see.'

Teacher: Tell me.

Kevin: Well, you know how when you hear things, you get sound-waves in your ears and they bounce off things so that you can hear them . . . when you see you send sightwaves out and they bounce back off things so you can see them.

After a short discussion and some demonstration by Kevin, who went round the classroom looking at things to show his teacher what was happening, the teacher suggested that he looked out of the window.

Teacher: What can you see?

Kevin: The playground, a tree, some people . . .

Teacher: Tap the glass. What's it like?

Kevin: Hard.

Teacher: If it is all hard, how can you see through it? Why doesn't it make your sightwaves bounce back and stop you seeing past?

Kevin: Oh.

Kevin did not seem to give it much further thought and soon had become reabsorbed in his other work. However, after lunch he returned to his teacher saying:

Kevin: I know how you see out of windows.

Teacher: How?

Kevin: Well the glass is really full of tiny holes that let the sightwaves past, but they are so small that you cannot see them.

This conversation is a modern version of the kind of exploratory talk pioneered by Susan Isaacs at the Malting House School in the 1930s. It is the kind of talk with which teachers feel comfortable. I doubt if Kevin's teacher wanted to offer a 'correct' scientific explanation to him since his own thinking had been at such a high cognitive level for a 6-year-old. The episode also illustrates the import-ance of allowing time for children to absorb information and transfer under-standing to a new area of enquiry.

But teachers do face real dilemmas about reconciling children's 'private' knowledge with the 'public' knowledge of Science. At what point *should* teachers begin to substitute 'scientific' explanations for the 'alternative frameworks' devised from children's 'common-sense' understandings and explanations? Or shall we know, as parents do when their children begin to question the Great Father Christmas Lie, when it is appropriate to offer each child the stark reality of 'scientific' explanations.

The foundation subjects

History and geography

There has been concern that rigour in teaching history and geography in primary schools has been forfeited in the name of topic work. The Schools Council project directed by Alan Blyth, *Place, Time and Society* (W. A. L. Blyth *et al.* 1976) focused on core concepts, skills and attitudes for the teaching of social sciences in primary schools, but the project was targeted at 8–13-year-olds. A follow-up project based in ILEA produced some excellent cross-cultural materials (ILEA 1978; 1979; 1980) but again focused on the junior age range. Joan Blyth's work on history and geography teaching in the early years (J. E. Blyth 1984) has been an influential resource for infant teachers. Increasingly issues like Peace Studies, Anti-Racist Education, Health Studies, World Studies and Links with Industry, emanating from various vested interests, have also attached themselves to the social studies curriculum of primary schools. It has been difficult for teachers to keep track of all these new initiatives, some of which such as Economic and Industrial Understanding and Environmental Education have now been identified within NCC documentation as cross-curricular themes.

A damning report by HMI (DES 1989c) on the state of history and geography teaching in primary schools, based on their inspection of 285 schools between 1982 and 1986, stated that

> most primary schools do not provide challenging historical and geo-graphical work for their pupils. In too many schools, too little time is devoted to these subjects; they are poorly planned and taught, and assessment is superficial or non-existent.
>
> (DES 1989c: 24)

The content of history and geography covered can depend quite arbitrarily on what historic buildings or geographical features crop up on school trips year by year.

The report also suggests that teachers may be underestimating the abilities of young children in history and geography. They argue,

> It is increasingly apparent that, for example, ideas associated with change, chronology, location and distribution can be understood by young children at an appropriate level if experienced in a practical way and within a context which makes sense to them.
>
> (DES 1989c: 26)

It is interesting, for example, that mapping, believed to be far too abstract a concept for young children, has been successfully introduced to 3–4-year-olds in the context of playing with model cars, buildings, animals, etc. on floor mats. The children have subsequently recorded the position of the objects, buildings, roads, rivers and railway lines on paper in the beginnings of mapping skills (Spencer *et al.* 1990). The children have been encouraged to develop their skills by mapping their own classroom and school environment, and then by mapping the immediate locality of the school playground and surrounding streets. The Final Report of the Geography Working Group proposes that children at Key Stage 1 will be expected to develop understanding of their immediate locality, of the UK and of Europe and the wider world. There are seven attainment targets. The first, Geographical Skills, underpins the content attainment targets. Skills to be learned include the use of maps and diagrams, fieldwork skills and the use of secondary sources. Attainment targets 2 to 4 – The home area and region, The United Kingdom within the European Community, The wider world – will require schools to collect a bank of resources such as local large scale ordnance survey maps, photographs of places in Europe and the wider world, videos and books with factual unbiased accounts of life-styles in other countries. It will help if the children and their families are drawn into the collection of these resources. It makes sense to draw on their experiences of holidays, places where the families used to live, countries of origin of grandparents etc. Attainment targets 5 and 6 – Physical and Human Geography – should be systematically taught as data from field trips, with maps, simple atlases, photographs, rock and soil samples, artefacts etc. used to explore basic concepts of physical and human geography. Finally attainment target 7, Environmental Geography, gives opportunities to tackle a range of 'green' issues. The use and misuse of natural resources and the possibilities of protecting and managing environments can be practised at a meaningful local level with young children – how to control litter, how to conserve plants and wildlife (in rural and urban settings), how to recycle school and domestic waste.

The Interim Report from the history working party proposed two profile components – historical understanding and historical investigation and analysis. There has been some dispute about how much emphasis should be placed on the content of the curriculum – factual knowledge about historical events – and how much on the processes of historical enquiry. There has also been some political pressure on the working group to ensure that British history is given precedence over European or world history. Happily, at Key Stage 1, it is suggested that children simply concentrate on basic questions such as 'Who am I?' and 'When and where am I?' in relation to information about their families, or collected from stories, or television and radio broadcasts about current local, national or international events.

Technology

Technology was the first foundation subject to be introduced to 5-year-olds. The Working Party divided the subject into two profile components – design and technology capability and information technology capability. Infant teachers were alarmed at the prospect of teaching a completely new area of the curriculum, but in fact many of the practical activities in early years education – construction play, modelling buildings and vehicles, making puppets, musical instruments, costumes and masks for performances, as well as the setting up of 'systems' such as school post offices, shops, the monitoring of arrangements for playtimes and dinner-times etc. – could form the basis of a cross-curricular approach to Technology at Key Stage 1.

The Working Party took a broad and liberal view of what constitutes technology. They argued in the Foreword to the programmes of study that

> Technology is the one subject in the National Curriculum that is directly concerned with generating ideas, making and doing. In emphasising the importance of practical capability, and providing opportunities for pupils to develop their powers to innovate, to make decisions, to create new solutions, it can play a unique role. Central to this role is the task of providing balance in a curriculum based on academic subjects – a balance in which the creative and practical capabilities of pupils can be fully developed and inter-related.
>
> (NCC/WO 1989e: 7)

Like teachers, young children can often express their intelligence more readily in doing than in explaining or recording what they have done! Perhaps the legislation for the advent of Technology into infant classrooms in September 1990 will give teachers a chance to pay some sustained attention to children involved in 'making and doing' activities without feeling guilty about not listening to readers or marking another page of a child's Scottish Primary Maths workbook.

Of course, the official view of the value placed on Technology is more instrumental. In the Foreword, the argument continues, 'Whilst the contribution of technology to the personal development of individuals is very important, of equal importance is its role in helping pupils to respond to the employment needs of business and industry' (NCC/WO 1989e: 7). It is one example of the many references to economics, consumerism and the world of work that permeate DES documentation after a decade of Thatcherism.

A positive aspect of the working party's approach to Technology is that it presents the subject as one that empowers girls and boys with a sense of their own practical capabilities and acknowledges that thinking and doing are mutually dependent processes. The Working Party have thus given equal status to four attainment targets within the design and technology profile component: Identifying needs and opporunities, Generating a design proposal, Planning and making, and Appraising. In the first set of proposals, they argued that 'These activities are not intended to represent separable stages in a linear process. They feed both forward and back into each other' (NCC/WO 1989d: 2.4). The Working Party acknowledged that with pupils at Key Stage 1 their experiences of handling and working with materials would often be the starting point for design and technological activities. For a young child, working with a pile of building blocks might be the process by which an understanding of basic structures begins to emerge; making a device which stops her pencils rolling on to the floor might be the beginning of understanding how human beings can design artefacts which make life more convenient for themselves; observing carefully and drawing classroom equipment – brushes, scissors, balances, clamps – might help to develop awareness of which materials are best suited to which functions.

This seems to be a more fruitful concept of technology in primary schools – and certainly more girl-friendly – than adult-imposed exercises in Technical Lego, making scale model vehicles out of ready-cut card triangles or balsa wood pieces or egg race challenges. There is already evidence (see Hughes 1986) that young girls are socialized into a lack of confidence in using computers. The kind of play experiences offered to boys will almost certainly give them an advantage if technology in primary schools is simply a downward extension of the male-dominated secondary school CDT. Primary teachers must be ready to resist this danger, because it is likely that the in-service opportunities offered to them will be fronted by secondary school trained, probably male, technology specialists.

Restricted access to computers is still a limitation to what infant teachers and children can achieve in information technology. Often the one school computer will be available to a class only for blocks of the school week or year. This constraint makes it very difficult for both teachers and children to use the computer in the way the interim report recommends (NCC/WO 1989d), that is that every 5-year-old 'should be able to work with a computer' from virtually the first day in school and that it should be used as part of normal daily classroom work across the curriculum – for the practice of literacy and numeracy skills, for storing and retrieving data and for word processing.

The arts and physical education

The arts and physical education are likely to be presented in a different way from other foundation subjects. Paragraph 24 of the Consultative Document on the National Curriculum (DES 1987) reads: 'For art, music and physical education there will be guidelines rather than specific attainment targets'. Dance is to be squeezed into the physical education curriculum, and drama, along with media studies, was included in the brief of the English working party!

Art

The Gulbenkian Report (Robinson 1982) on the arts in schools presented cogent arguments for the entitlement of all children to quality arts education throughout their schooling. However, the fact that the arts, with physical education, will be the last foundation subjects to be introduced within the

National Curriculum programme indicates that the status of these subjects is still low. Few primary schools have written guidelines for the teaching of art and music. This is particularly unfortunate because many teachers feel as insecure about teaching the arts as they do about teaching science.

In fact, in the visual arts in infant classrooms, art is rarely taught, but rather allowed to happen. It happens beyond the regular boundaries of the teacher's working space, perhaps in wet areas in new or refurbished buildings or in cloakroom or corridor spaces converted as messy areas in older school buildings. Art activities may be set up by the teacher but they are often supervised by nursery assistants or parent helpers, and are included within 'choosing' time, the 'play' rather than 'work' component of the day. Teacher attention is only sporadically paid to creative activities, particularly where there is a 'rotating groups' system of organization. It is rare to find a teacher planning methodically to cover a range of media over a term or year, or systematically teaching the use of tools and techniques other than in short introductory sessions. So, for example, children might be given general instructions about the art activity for that day during the start of the day 'mat time' – 'I want you to paint some lovely pictures about Spring today,' or 'Today we'll be making some buildings from the boxes on the table over there', or 'Choose some nice material to stick on the horses for our circus frieze'. But unless teachers timetable themselves to spend time interacting with the children while they work on the tasks, how can they teach basic techniques of colour mixing, which brushes are most appropriate for painting the sky and which for blossoms; which boxes are the most appropriate shapes for making bungalows, flats, semi-detached houses, and the techniques of covering boxes with paper so that children can then begin to think about the detailing of roofs, windows, doors, brickwork, guttering; find pictures of horses by a range of artists to look and see how you can convey the form and texture of those marvellous animals . . . ?

If children are to progress in the visual arts, they need to be *taught* the techniques of how to draw, paint, model, weave and pot. But many teachers still cling to the view that art is something mysteriously innate and that teaching somehow interferes with a creative process. On the contrary, I believe that children cannot be free to be expressive until they have mastered basic skills in representing their feelings and ideas in line, colour, texture or form. I do not believe that we should make a distinction between teaching children to read and write and teaching them to paint and draw.

Children also need to be taught that to succeed in creating the effects they want may take many attempts. Even young children may have to go back several times to a painting or drawing or model before it is complete. A problem identified by HMI (DES 1978a) is that children are offered perhaps too many instant 'Blue Peter style' art experiences that produce a product, without sustained attention to the processes within the learning experience. This leads to children working in a superficial way. Children need to familiarise themselves with the characteristics of particular materials and to acquire some degree of mastery over essential skills and techniques. A more carefully selected range of art and craft activities, worked at more thoroughly, would enable children to reach higher standards in the execution of their work and obtain more satisfaction from it.

(DES 1978a: 5.94)

There are opportunities for teachers to draw on the expertise of local artists and craftspeople to demonstrate the use of particular media and techniques under the auspices of Artists in Residence schemes funded by some LEAs. All schools should be able to build up a stock of art books, posters, postcards, advertisements, and videos of artists at work, both popular and traditional, from a wide range of cultures. These resources can provide support for teachers who feel 'inept' themselves at art, and therefore anxious about teaching it. They also open up to children a whole world of visual literacy and encourage them to see art as a vital part of living culture, rather than something set apart for an elite section of the community.

Finally, work in the visual arts in primary schools has often degenerated into a servicing agency for the window dressing of a school, with disastrous results for the quality of art teaching and learning. Headteachers and their staff know that schools are often judged by visitors on the 'quality' of their displays. Often, without any account being taken of the educational experiences being offered to the children, teachers feel compelled to spend many hours planning and directing the creation of elaborate friezes for the hall, corridors or their classrooms display boards. Sometimes, particularly in new school buildings, the amount of display space they are told they are 'responsible for' is enough to produce severe stress in new teachers before they ever catch sight of their pupils! It must be time to call a halt to this nonsense. Surely displays should simply be of a range of children's current writing, art work, scientific and mathematical activities – simply mounted, at child height – for the *children* to share in each other's learning experiences. Some boards should be available, like the pinboards in many kitchens, for informal exchanges of information, reminders, lists, notes for use by children and adults. Set alongside children's work should be teacher stimuli or practical support for learning – instructions about feeding pets, number lines, lists of new vocabulary, pictures or posters reflecting a current area of interest for the class, photographs of the latest school trip. All this should be displayed with quiet professionalism rather than window-dressing hype.

Music

On the whole the teaching of music in primary schools has been given guarded approval by HMI reports. When asked by HMI, most headteachers appeared to have a clear view of the kinds of music activities that should be offered to

children in primary schools. HMI (DES 1978a) quote a typical response from a
headteacher:

> Children should have experience of sound and rhythm in music through
> listening and through participation. They should have the opportunity to
> experience music through movement, singing and the use of tuned and
> untuned percussion instruments.
>
> (DES 1978a, 5.96: 66)

There is often a music specialist within a primary school who takes each class
for music during the week. Non-specialists have relied on the excellent school
broadcasts for support in teaching new songs with basic musical accompani-
ment. Singing has been regularly taught – particularly in the context of
practising songs for assemblies, or the more public performances of school
concerts. Many infant classrooms have music corners where children can
experiment with sounds, though this provision is often hard to reconcile with
the need to keep noise levels manageable.

Many parents are keen for their children to learn to play instruments. Some
local authorities have in the past provided excellent services both in the loan of
instruments to pupils, and in a range of peripatetic support teachers to teach
wind and string instruments to interested or gifted children. It is interesting to
speculate why music, rather than the visual arts or dance, has managed to gain
this level of financial support. What is unclear now is how local authorities and
schools will manage to pay the bills for specialist music teaching within the
constraints of local financial management of schools. Sadly if the costs are
passed on to parents, the entitlement of children to learn an instrument within
school may be lost. Some parents will simply not be able to afford tuition fees.

Physical education
There has been growing anxiety about the poor state of physical fitness of many
school children in the UK. At a time in their lives when physical development is
critical, there are simply not enough opportunities for children to exercise
their bodies and develop their capabilities. Access to safe outdoor play in the
inner cities or even on suburban streets is limited. In nursery schools and
classes it is possible to offer young children opportunities to play on large
outdoor equipment in the safety of fenced and supervised spaces. However, for
the 4-year-olds in reception classes, as for many infant children, physical
exercise within school may be limited to a couple of hall times per week. The
hall space has to serve many functions – for school dinners, fund-raising
activities, television broadcasts, rehearsal space for school concerts, the venue
for visiting theatre groups – the list is endless. All these functions may further
limit the time available to young children in the hall for physical education and
of course physical education outdoors is restricted by the vagaries of the British
climate.

It is usual for primary teachers to have one large apparatus lesson each week, and at least one other timetabled session focused on dance/movement, small apparatus equipment or outdoor games. In dance HMI found (DES 1978a) that three-fifths of the teachers of 7-year-olds were using BBC programmes as the basis for dance/movement lessons. In using balls, hoops, beanbags, etc, teachers generally expected children to practise in pairs or small groups the skills of throwing, catching, kicking and hitting. In floor work in the hall space, teachers concentrated on developing children's awareness and skills in body movements such as balancing, jumping, hopping, etc. Finally HMI suggested that 'full advantage was not always taken of fine weather' to use outdoor space for physical education. It seems sensible that the PE timetable should vary with the seasons in the UK, but many schools continue doggedly with the same routines of timetabled hall and outdoor games activities winter and summer alike!

Unless there is strong direction from a school policy, some teachers may not even take advantage of their few timetabled physical education slots! It takes a great deal of energy and patience to organize a class of 4–5-year-olds into changing into their t-shirts and shorts – particularly if there is no ancillary help for thirty sets of buttons, zips, shoe-laces and socks – and to prepare the equipment for a lesson all within a half-hour slot. A further difficulty for non-specialist teachers is that many schools do not have written guidelines for physical education (DES 1982a). It is thus hard for teachers to challenge the more able children or to ensure progression across all ability levels. HMI reported 'There was evidence of some children being insufficiently challenged; they were unresponsive, sometimes lethargic, sometimes noisy and uncontrolled, and there was a lack of progression in the work' (DES 1982a: para 2.161). It is against this background that the Working Party in Physical Education will be drawing up 'guidelines' or perhaps programmes of study.

Most arts and PE practitioners are now anxious that their subjects should be treated in the same way as other foundation subjects. They are lobbying for programmes of study and statements of attainment. They fear that anything less will present a risk of the low status of these areas of the curriculum being perpetuated.

Religious education

Under the terms of the Education Act 1944, religious education was obligatory, but there was a conscience clause whereby teachers might opt out of teaching the subject and parents might remove their children from religious education classes in voluntary aided or maintained schools. Local authorities were required to provide an Agreed Syllabus in RE.

In 1982 HMI reported that 'popular Bible stories, often in a random order' or 'stories associated with the main Christian festivals' formed the basis of 'the traditional approach' to RE teaching in many First Schools. Indeed, although RE figured in teachers' curriculum planning, there was little evidence of RE teaching in many classrooms and assemblies often became 'the main vehicle for religious education in the school' (DES 1982a).

The trend in schools had been to broaden teaching religion into teaching about religions, particularly in areas of the country where many faiths were represented within the school community. In some schools, assemblies had become almost entirely secular in character – opportunities to create and sustain a school culture, to share work across age ranges and classes, to invite parents to class assemblies based around the children's current topic work.

Under the terms of the Education Reform Act 1988, religious education is termed a 'basic' rather than foundation subject. It will not have programmes of study and attainment targets. Agreed syllabuses must be reviewed by local Standing Advisory Councils on RE (SACREs) and must 'reflect the fact that the religious traditions in Great Britain are in the main Christian whilst taking account of the teaching and practices of other principal religions represented in Great Britain'. The membership of the SACREs who will draw up the syllabuses must represent 'such Christian and other religious denominations as, in the opinion of the authority, will appropriately reflect the principal religious traditions in the area'.

Daily acts of collective worship are obligatory and the majority of these should be 'wholly or mainly of a broadly Christian character'. It is possible for schools with, for example, a predominantly Hindu or Muslim population to apply to the SACREs for exemption from this requirement, but there is no reference made to accommodating the beliefs of a predominantly non-religious community.

The fact that our laws require us to teach religious education within a secular school system is something of surprise to many outsiders to the British education system. The fact that it was the *only* subject we were required by law to teach under the terms of the Education Act 1944 was a source of genuine amusement. However, it may be a particular anxiety for teachers and parents that young children should be drawn into an 'in the main Christian' religious education when they have little understanding of their right to opt out.

The National Curriculum and planning the infant curriculum

Secondary school teachers simply have to wait for the Orders for their own subject to be presented in a ritzy National Curriculum Council plastic-backed ring folder and get on with arguing about and/or teaching the contents. Pity the poor primary teachers who, in their capacity as class teachers, have to come to terms with every one of the subjects (apart from modern languages) as they roll off the NCC production line. When all the Orders are complete, primary teachers will have to be aware of a vast number of statements of attainment when they tackle their overall planning for a year. How are they going to cope?

If we return to the process model of curriculum planning set out in Figure 4 (p. 96), we can see how some examples of attainment targets from the programmes of study can be mapped on to the diagram. Supposing ROCKS is taken as the starting-point for half a term's planning. The 'what' and the 'how' of the curriculum can be mapped into the model as shown in Figure 5.

The specific statements of attainment used to illustrate the point are drawn from the three core subjects, but the overall planning is cross-curricular. They are at Level 2, the level at which most 7-year-olds will be expected to function after two years' experience of the National Curriculum.

1 Maths – Attainment Target 8: Measures
• Use non-standard measures in length, area, volume, capacity, weight and time to compare objects and recognise the need to use standard units
• Know the most commonly used units in length, capacity, 'weight', and time and what they are used for
(*Mathematics in the National Curriculum*, NCC/WO 1989b: 21)
2 Science – Attainment Target 6: Types and Uses of Materials
• Be able to recognise important similarities and differences, including hardness, flexibility and transparency, in the characteristics of materials
• Be able to group materials according to their characteristics
(*Science in the National Curriculum*, NCC/WO 1989c: 14)

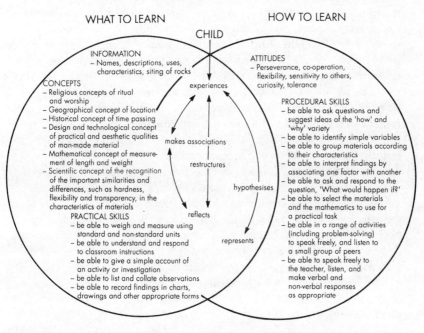

Figure 5 A content and process model for the National Curriculum.
Source: Anning and Gates 1989: 27

3 English – Attainment Target 1: Speaking and Listening
   • Participate as speakers and listeners in a group engaged in a given task
   • Describe an event, real or imagined, to the teacher or another pupil
   • Listen attentively to stories and poems, and talk about them
   • Talk with the teacher, listen and ask and answer questions
   • Respond appropriately to a range of more complex instructions given by a
     teacher, and give simple instructions
                    (*English in the National Curriculum*, NCC/WO 1989a: 3)

Rocks and stones might be collected by or made available to the children
for initial discussions. Visits might be made to sites including natural
rocks and manufactured building/construction materials (e.g. beach,
countryside, waste land, building site, shopping centre). From group
discussion (English), children may begin to consider ways of describing
similarities and differences in the materials they observe – colour, shape,
surface texture, weight, size (Science). This could lead to children
representing their findings in a variety of ways – for example, observa-
tional drawings of stones and rocks in varying conditions and situations,
descriptive writing, photographs – all of which help develop the skills of
observation and classification. From these sensory explorations, children
may move on to devising experiments involving fair tests on rocks. What
would happen if we tried to build with various materials, weighed them,
made marks on and with them, used them in conjunction with other
materials in a variety of conditions? Children might, for example, see how
many or what weight of bricks, pebbles, pumice stones, concrete, etc.,
would tear given supermarket paper – or plastic – carrier bags. What
happens to different kinds of rocks when they are put into water? How do
they change in appearance and weight, and how much water do they
displace? Results involving weight, length and displacement properties
might be tabulated in mathematical form, initially in non standard units,
but, through collaboration and comparison of results, the need for
standard units would soon emerge. (Maths)
    Geographical and historical perspectives would emerge from a dis-
cussion of the sites. Reference books would be a valuable source of
additional information. Story books and poetry chosen to complement
the theme of rocks would stimulate the children's imaginations and
perhaps lead to dance, drama, music and visual art. The study of carvings
and shrines could also encourage children to talk about sacred rituals
and forms of worship. The possibilities are endless, and using this
cross-curricular approach it is possible to identify a wide range of aspects
of learning from the National Curriculum attainment targets and incorporate them into the model.
                                            (Anning and Gates 1989: 27)

Over a year, and in consultation with colleagues, teachers could build up a sequence of units of planning, much as they have done in the past with topic webs, but with the content more rigorously defined and processes more clearly planned for. It may be that each half term during a school year might have a different major curriculum emphasis – technology, history, geography, music, art, physical education – while the core subjects would run consistently throughout the year's planning. Some attainment targets may have to be taught separately outside a topic framework if this proves to be the most effective way to ensure coverage across Key Stages. Topic work should be seen as a device to ensure cohesion and continuity in curriculum planning, but not as a strait-jacket.

While infant teachers struggle to come to terms with the mechanics of implementing the programmes of study, they are also deeply concerned about assessment at Key Stage 1, planning for children with special educational needs, and with the knock-on effects of the National Curriculum on the quality of education offered to children in nursery and reception classes. It is to these and other related issues that we turn in the final chapter.

6
Into the new ERA

Will the wide-ranging requirements of the Education Reform Act really herald a new era? We have already seen that the prescribed curriculum content for the core subjects – English, Mathematics and Science – are reassuringly in line with what has been defined as 'good practice' in primary education. There is a strong emphasis on practical and collaborative work and a recognition of the kinds of research findings reported in Chapter 2 on the way children learn.

It is, however, significant that the pecking order for the implementation of the Orders reflects the more worrying aspects of the primary school curriculum identified in previous chapters of the book, with the 'low status' subjects – the arts and physical education – tagged on to the end of the programme for the implementation of a National Curriculum.

Then there is the worry about the sheer amount of curriculum coverage teachers are legally required to deliver. Infant teachers are already finding the task of covering the attainment targets in Mathematics, Science and English difficult enough. There is a real anxiety that an infant school National Curriculum will become so overcrowded that pupils will be rushed through areas of experience and learning in order that their 'progress' through statements of attainment can be recorded. There are already signs that DES officials are backing off what has been prescribed in the NCC documentation, with mutterings of 'too detailed' and 'too prescriptive' being heard as the resource and staffing implications of the legislation for schools begin to become a reality rather than pious hopes on pieces of paper. The unequal distribution of time and resources between the basics, the core subjects, and the rest may simply be perpetuated, particularly if only the core subjects are to be assessed by standard assessment tasks at the end of Key Stage 1. And how much time will be left for the kind of spontaneous response to children's interests or teachers' enthusiasms that has often been the hallmark of the most lively infant educa-tion? It would be a pity if the curriculum became dull and lifeless in the name of rigour.

It has been acknowledged that the core and foundation subjects simply provide a 'scaffolding' for the design of the school curriculum. NCC have also identified a range of *dimensions* (such as personal and social education), cross-curricular *skills* (such as study, communication and problem-solving skills) and *themes* (such as health education, citizenship and economic/industrial understanding), which schools will also be expected to cover in their overall curriculum planning. The framework provided by a National Curricu-lum 5–16 *should* ensure that the discrepancies in children's access to areas of learning and experience in different school and classroom contexts across the country will be systematically addressed. In theory all children now have a legal entitlement to a broad and balanced and coherent education throughout the period of their formal education. The 'breadth and balance' of curriculum coverage in all schools is likely to be monitored by paper exercises such as the curriculum audit forms currently circulated to all schools. Headteachers are required to go through the lengthy procedure of identifying the number of hours each year group will devote to various aspects of the curriculum. It is assumed that the paper exercise will be monitored in practice by LEA or HMI inspections of schools.

Assessment

More worrying for headteachers and teachers are the implications of the monitoring of pupil progress and, by implication, school effectiveness, through the assessment procedures which will be required of schools. The innovative report by the National Curriculum Task Group on Assessment and Testing (TGAT) (DES 1988a) presented a complex model for the assessment of pupils' progression through the National Curriculum.

In the report it was proposed that daily teacher assessments should operate alongside the formal assessment procedures controlled by the Schools Ex-aminations and Assessment Council (SEAC). Four purposes of assessment were identified: *formative* and *diagnostic* (both of which have a feed forward function in planning the appropriate learning experiences and activities for pupils), *summative* (which gives information about the overall achievements of pupils at the end of a defined period of learning), and *evaluative* (which, like the kind of APU testing to which we have become accustomed, gives informa-tion about some specific aspects of the work of a school or LEA). The authors of the report make the following recommendations:

> We recommend that the basis of the national assessment system be essentially formative, but designed also to indicate where there is a need

for more detailed diagnostic assessment. At age 16, however, it should incorporate assessment with summative functions.

(DES 1988a: para 27)

All this sounds very reasonable. The assumption is that teachers will continue to use 'normal' day-to-day assessment procedures in classrooms – taking account of the outcomes of children's learning activities, observing children on tasks, and utilizing feedback gained from interaction with them to monitor and record their progress.

It is as well to remember, however, the evidence that N. Bennett *et al.* (1984) offered about the difficulty infant teachers appear to have in diagnosing children's levels of attainment (see pp. 81–3). It is also worth remembering at this point that teachers who worked on a follow-up in-service programme within the research project found that the main obstacle to refining their skills in assessing and diagnosing children's learning was lack of sufficient time to work in depth with individual pupils. The TGAT Report recognizes the complexity involved in assessing and recording children's progress across the curriculum and recommends that an extensive programme of in-service should be planned to help teachers to refine their skills in assessment. It is also becoming apparent that primary teachers will need non-contact time – perhaps thirty minutes a day – in order to be able to focus on the skills and procedures of assessment and to keep records up to date. Recent HMI statements have hinted that primary teachers may be allocated 10 per cent of their school time as non-contact time.

The first extensive 'packs' of training materials, published by SEAC, were delivered to all teachers, students in training, advisory staff and tutors involved in initial training in January 1990 (SEAC 1989b). The materials provide a framework of activities within which teachers can begin to refine their strategies for observing, making judgements about and recording children's progress through the ten levels of each set of attainment targets. There are lists of the statements of attainment which would best be assessed by children operating individually, in groups or as a class. There is advice about which statements of a child's attainment may be assessed by looking at the outcome of an activity, and which by observing a child actually doing an activity.

However, there are all kinds of assumptions about teacher expertise implicit in an instruction from the pack such as:

> choose three statements of attainment which are likely to be covered by your lesson plan for tomorrow, three children who have just reached one or more of the Statements of Attainment, think about the specific features of performance which indicate that a child has demonstrated the attainment, and record the evidence.

(SEAC 1989b: Activity B, Pack A)

Moreover, some of the statements of attainment are so vaguely defined that it is hard to know how the most competent teacher would make a judgement about whether a child had 'achieved' them. For example, if a teacher were assessing whether a child had achieved Level 2, AT 2, English: 'read a range of material with some independence, fluency, accuracy and understanding', how should the teacher define 'a range of material', and what should s/he understand by 'some' independence, fluency, etc. In assessing whether a child had achieved Level 2, AT 1, Maths: 'select the materials and the mathematics to use for a task', would one example of this achievement be enough to say that the child had reached this level of attainment or should the child have demonstrated competence across a range of mathematical activities? There are many difficulties still to be resolved in the implementation of a criterion referenced system of assessment in our UK primary school context. It is still very unfamiliar territory to teachers whose experience of assessment has mostly been the norm-referenced standardized tests of reading and mathematics or general intelligence tests.

What does not sound reasonable to teachers are the proposals for a national system of assessment which will run alongside school-based procedures. The acronym SATs, for standard assessment tasks, strikes fear into the hearts of teachers of 7-year-olds. It is proposed that every child should undertake three SATs during the summer term of their final year in the infant school. The children will then have been working on the National Curriculum for approximately two years and they will be assumed to have reached the end of Key Stage 1. Three consortia – each comprising expertise from examination boards, centres of research, publishers and LEAs – were given contracts to pilot SATs for 7-year-olds in 1991. Their brief was to make test activities relate to the ten levels of attainment targets within the profile components of subjects areas (at the time of piloting only the three core subjects were available for them to work from). The tests were thus to be criterion referenced, that is related to what children had learnt during the previous two years. They were designed 'to establish what children know, understand and can do' (DES 1989d: para 41). They are *not* like the norm-referenced reading, IQ, or mathematics tests to which primary schools are accustomed.

The brief for the three consortia also specified that the test activities were to be as near normal classroom practice as possible, and the schools able to select from a bank of SATs those that appeared to be appropriate for their school context, pupils, curriculum coverage, classroom management style, etc. One of the consortia planned activities which were assessed within the process of a complete topic for a half-term's work. One consortia required teachers to select the level of task appropriate for each child. Another planned to have similar tasks presented to all children so that each child could progress as far as they were able to on the tasks. These two principles are called differentiation by task and differentiation by outcome. The third consortia intended to use a mixture of these two principles! The assumption was that the most workable system was to be selected for the first unreported run of SATs in 1991. All three consortia ran into difficulties in trialling proposed SATs. The amount of time it took to assess all 7-year-olds in a class in all the core subject profile components appalled many teachers in the schools used for testing. The final versions of SATs are likely to be considerably 'trimmed' from original TGAT intentions and will utilize a limited number of attainment targets for testing. The first reported run is to be in 1992.

The results of children's performance on SATs will be set alongside the 'normal' teacher assessments of the children's capabilities. Infant teachers will have to have completed their normal assessment procedures by the end of the spring term before the SATs are administered. The SATs will be administered in the first half of the summer term. The TGAT Report suggested that teacher assessments should take preference over the results of the SATs. However, in a document sent from SEAC to the DES (SEAC 1989a), it was suggested that 'The SAT assessment is ... preferred to TA (Teacher Assessment) where it is available', and that 'the SAT results, where available, should be used for recording and reporting purposes, instead of TA, except where this makes a change of profile component result which the teacher wishes to query'.

The TGAT Report recommended that groups of schools should send teacher representatives to moderation meetings where discrepancies between individual school scores and difficulties over individual pupil ratings would be addressed. Although this process was recognized to be time-consuming, the authors believed that teachers would gain enormous professional benefits from open discussions of their pupils' learning outcomes and progress with colleagues from other schools. The TGAT Report emphasized the importance of upgrading and supporting the professional judgements in assessment of the teachers who work daily with 7-year-olds. The stance implied in the SEAC document negates this principle. The message is that in the end it is the test result, rather than the judgement of the teacher that is to be given the higher status. In view of the difficulties in the SAT trials, the 'experts' may well have to reverse the decision yet again.

Information about children's progress through the attainment targets is to be reported to parents at the end of each school year and the results of their performance on the SATs at the end of Key Stages. Parents will receive information about their children's performance on profile components rather than on individual statements of attainment. It is proposed that the results of pupils' individual SATs scores should be aggregated to give a mean score for the cohort of pupils in each school. The TGAT Report recommended that the aggregated test results of 7-year-olds should *not* be made public. However, government sources have indicated that schools will be strongly advised to do so. There is the inevitable worry that schools will be held publicly accountable for the test results of 7-year-olds without any account being taken of the 'baseline' positions at age 5 of a particular cohort of children in a school population. At later Key Stage testing points – at 11, 14 and 16 – there will of course be the previous Key Stage results to which reference may be made. In other words, Key Stage 2, 3 and 4 schools might feel that they were being judged more fairly on how far they had moved a cohort of children from one clearly identified point on a continuum to another.

The anxiety of teachers of 7-year-olds is understandable. It has prompted a number of primary schools to investigate their own systems of baseline testing of 5-year-olds. This may have the unfortunate consequence of children being subjected to a battery of 'formal' tests as they enter the National Curriculum at 5. Not a happy prospect on the eve of one's fifth birthday! There is even the worrying prospect of pre-fives being 'tested' as they register for a school place – a procedure already established in some independent schools. Some head-teachers will not welcome children who are likely to depress the aggregated test results of the school. Is it possible that in some schools those who do not make the grade at school entry point will be told that the school has no place for them?

Aside from this kind of hysteria, common sense dictates that in most schools it will be useful to have information about what the 5-year-old at official entry point to the National Curriculum can do. This should avoid the practice of every child being put through 'readiness' programmes whatever their previous experiences and competencies. But a much sounder alternative to 'testing' at 5 must be for schools to work with nursery staff, playground leaders and parents to compile some kind of pupil profile for children starting school. An interesting example of such a system is the booklet *All About Me* compiled by Sheila Wolfendale (1989). Parents and adult workers involved in the care and education of young children are encouraged to talk with them about their achievements. For example practical competencies such as being able to dress and undress without help or ride a bike are recorded. There are also sections on for example 'My Moods and Feelings' (an area which would need to be handled with great sensitivity) and 'Language Development'. Working in this collaborative way with parents right from the beginnings of schooling may make it easier for teachers to communicate more openly and honestly with parents about the child's progress in school.

There is evidence that parents do *not* at present get accurate information about their children's capabilities through the conventional school processes of parents' evenings (Tizard *et al.* 1988: ch. 5) or school reports. In Tizard's study 'the majority of parents had received no information on their child's relative progress and fewer black than white parents had been given feedback by teachers'. Teachers told the researchers that they did not like to give this kind of information to parents 'because they did not like to label or compare children' (Tizard *et al.* 1988: 91). Given the sensitivity amongst the teaching profession to the dangers of self-fulfilling prophecies, this reluctance is understandable. But surely parents *do* have a right to have more accurate information about their children's progress in school. To date we have managed to get away with a certain vagueness – 'She's doing fine' or 'He's not quite ready for reading yet' – but the new legislation will require teachers to be much more specific about what children can and cannot do; this requirement will mean that teachers have to keep detailed records to show 'the attainment targets covered by each pupil' (NCC 1989a: 16).

What would be singularly *unhelpful* would be the presentation of the results of detailed assessments to parents without any explanation as to what the numbers, attainment target levels, profile components and associated jargon actually means! Communicating with parents is another area where there is a desperate need for training teachers – both at initial and in-service levels. As acronyms proliferate, the restricted code amongst educators becomes more and more dense and inaccessible. We must not forget that for many more fortunate people SATs, Attainment Targets, NCC and SEAC are meaningless strings of letters.

Special educational needs

The Education Act 1981 redefined the role that LEAs and schools were to play in the education of children with special educational needs. The Act reflected recommendations within the influential Warnock Report (DES 1978b) that as far as possible children with special educational needs should be integrated with rather than separated from pupils in mainstream schools. The Warnock Report indicated that there is likely to be a notional 2 per cent of the school population whose needs would be sufficiently specialized to warrant a process defined as 'statementing'. The framework within which children should be 'statemented' was set out within Circular 1/83 (DES 1983). The process involves full parental consultation and is usually co-ordinated within LEAs by educational psychologists. The LEA is required to provide resources to meet the particular defined needs of statemented children.

A larger group of children, a further 18 per cent of the school population according to the Warnock Report, are expected to qualify as having 'a learning difficulty which calls for special education provision to be made' (para 1 (1) of the Education Act 1981). The Act defines a child over 5 years old who has learning difficulties as one who has

a significantly greater difficulty in learning than the majority of children his age; or he has a disability which either prevents or hinders him from making use of educational facilities of a kind generally provided in schools, within the area of the local authority concerned, for children of his age.

(Education Act 1981: Section 1(2))

Policy statements on special educational needs are clear, but there is evidence that the practice of these policies is patchy. It is dependent upon both LEA commitment and school expertise (Hegarty *et al.* 1981). Some LEAs invest money and time into screening procedures across the whole population to identify children who qualify for additional resourcing (see for example ILEA's

Classroom Observation Profile for infant teachers: Goldstein *et al.* 1984). When children have been identified as having special needs LEAs adopt a range of strategies to accommodate those needs. For some children whose needs cannot be met in mainstream schooling, special school placements are provided. In some authorities children are attached to units within schools so that they can have specialized teaching for some of the school day, but are 'partially integrated' into the mainstream school for some aspects of school timetabling. In other situations additional teaching staff may be attached to schools to work alongside mainstream teachers, either within the classroom or withdrawing groups or individual children for specialized support. For particular children with defined physical needs (such as hearing or visual impairment or spina bifida) or behaviour difficulties (such as hyperactivity, aggression or severe withdrawal symptoms) or with acute learning difficulties, full time non-teaching assistants may be employed to work with the child in a mainstream classroom.

Though most infant teachers are sympathetic towards the ideology of integration enshrined in the Warnock Report, in practice at school and classroom operational level, there are problems in implementing the ideology. The first difficulty arises right at the identification point of children's special educational needs from teachers' reluctance (already referred to in Chapter 3) to label children as 'different'. This reluctance is particularly acute when the label implies 'of lower ability' – hence the range of euphemisms teachers adopt in describing such children – 'takes a long time to catch on', 'a slow learner'. But to go as far as to 'statement' children is perceived as assigning an extreme label to them. Therefore there is a tendency for the staff to delay putting into motion the statementing procedures until the final year of infant schooling. The result of the delay, though well intentioned, can mean that children are deprived of specialist help and additional resources during the first three formative years of schooling. On the whole teachers are more ready to request statementing procedures for those children whose behaviour is so disruptive that they make life extremely difficult for both the teacher and the rest of the class. Physical disabilities are also quickly identified and attended to. It is the children with learning difficulties whom the teachers feel squeamish about identifying.

It is also fair to say that in some LEAs there are so little specialist support and resources made available to children with special educational needs, that headteachers have simply given up the unequal battle to have their rightful allocation of additional staffing or capitation as specified within the legal framework of the Act, and therefore delay putting into motion complicated and time-consuming statementing procedures.

If schools are assigned additional staff to support children with special educational needs, there are particular management issues to be addressed so that maximum benefit can be gained from their presence. The management issues arise at both school and classroom level. A headteacher must decide if it

is really legitimate to assign non-teaching assistants who have been employed
to support children with special educational needs to make the coffee and tea
for the teachers or to spend hours triple-mounting children's art work. A class
teacher must learn the skills, rarely acknowledged within initial or in-service
training, of working collaboratively with other professionals. They must also
recognize that it is not good enough simply to allow the pace of teaching/
learning interactions to slow down as extra adult help is fed into a classroom. In
other words the extra help needs a complete rethink rather than replication of
a style of classroom management. The strategies for effective team teaching
need careful and intelligent consideration both at personal and operational
levels.

The question of specialized expertise in the education of children with
special needs is another problem within infant schools. Many LEAs encourage a
policy whereby every school has a co-ordinator for special needs. Their role, as
with curriculum specialists, is to offer up-to-date expertise and advice to all
classroom teachers and to work alongside teachers to model effective teaching,
classroom management and record-keeping strategies. The problem is that
there are few in-service courses on offer to keep such co-ordinators informed
of the vast range of specialist knowledge that used to be centred on the now
rapidly diminishing special schools.

At initial training level, CATE criteria for the accreditation of teacher training
programmes include the specification that students should be given information and advice about teaching children with special educational needs.
However, as initial training is increasingly switched to the one-year primary
postgraduate courses rather than four-year BEd routes it becomes almost
impossible to allot sufficient hours, within an overcrowded PGCE timetable, to
cover adequately the complexity of identifying and responding to all manner of
special needs.

Of course, the rhetoric now is that *every* child has special needs. That is true
in so far that every person is an individual learner with particular life and
learning experiences. We have already tried to address the principle that each
individual pupil nevertheless manifests similar learning behaviours to those of
his or her classmates. But the fact is that within these generalized patterns of
similarities and differences, there is indeed the small percentage of children
who manifest a range of behaviours that teachers recognize as different enough
to warrant specialized teaching; there is also the category of gifted children to
recognize as having special educational needs.

It is unfortunate that the good intentions of the policy of integration may
result, for the reasons identified – lack of LEA commitment to providing
resources, lack of specialist expertise amongst experienced teachers, lack of
adequate training for new teachers – in children with special needs receiving
an inadequate education. It is also significant that it is only now in the 1990s that
researchers are beginning to ask the *children* with special educational needs
what their preferences are – for mainstreaming or integration.

How then can parents insist upon their children's rights to specialist support? For parents unfamiliar with the legislation and local provision for special educational needs, it can be a difficult process to put pressure on the school system. They have to rely for information upon particular headteachers, psychologists, and education officers. The advice parents are given may simply reflect an easy option for the LEA and local school system. That is why the Warnock Report recommended that an independent body should be available to which parents might go for unbiased advice.

The National Curriculum Council stress that from September 1990 all children are entitled to participate in the National Curriculum (NCC 1989e). They urge minimal use of the arrangements, through Sections 17–19 of the Education Reform Act, for exempting children: a process called 'disapplication'. If it *is* necessary to exempt children from the statutory requirements of curriculum coverage and assessment procedures, disapplication is to be seen as a temporary arrangement, not as fixed category for children, and where disapplication is agreed, an alternative curriculum for the children must be specified. Some children may take more time to progress through the curriculum. On the other hand gifted children may move very quickly through the levels of attainment for certain subjects or at certain times of their school careers. It is suggested that children may work with a class of older or younger children for some subjects if this seems appropriate, although it is stressed that there is no intention of keeping children 'down' or moving children 'up' on the basis of results in formal assessment only.

A National Curriculum and the pre-fives

In the document, *A Framework for the Primary Curriculum*, sent by NCC to all primary schools, there is a clear statement that 'To establish artificial boundaries between the education of children under five and that received by five year olds would be both counter-productive and an opportunity lost' (NCC 1989a: para 4.5). We know that 24 per cent of under-fives are in nursery schools or nursery classes, but access for pre-fives to nursery education is dependent on huge variations in LEA provision. Already 62 per cent of 4-year-olds in maintained schools are admitted early into reception classes (sometimes taken out of nursery classes while they are still 4, sometimes admitted straight from home or playgroup provision) (DES 1989e). Thus the UK school starting age is rapidly being established at a startling 4 years of age! HMI have stated that evidence they have collected from schools indicates that 'Taking all factors into account, children under five in nursery schools and classes generally receive a broader, better balanced education than those in primary classes' (HMI 1989a). In a survey of the quality of education for 4-year-olds in primary classes, they reported that 'For the majority of four year olds . . . there is an over-emphasis on some aspects of the basic skills of literacy and numeracy' and 'The educational purposes of play and investigative work are not sufficiently understood and provided for' (HMI 1989b). HMI also indicated that very few of the teachers they observed had been trained to work with the under-fives.

Whether the under-fives are in nursery or reception class contexts, it makes sense for staff to be aware of the requirements of the National Curriculum for 5-year-olds. Many of the statements of attainment for Level 1 are well within the achievement of some 4-year-olds, and indeed some 3-year-olds. For example the Science Attainment Target, Level 1, states that children should be able to 'Observe familiar materials and events in their immediate environment, at first hand, using their senses'. Neither Maria Montessori nor Susan Isaacs would have had misgivings about this attainment target within their nurseries. English Attainment Target 1, Speaking and Listening, states that children should be able to 'Listen attentively, and respond to stories and poems.' Mathematics attainment Target 10, Level 1, states that children should be able to 'Build with 3-D solid shapes and draw 2-D shapes and describe them, e.g. make various constructions from a range of materials'.

However, the vital proviso is that the *methods* by which children should be encouraged towards achievements should be based on 'children's interests and appetite for play, building upon these to achieve educational objectives which complement, and have much in common with, the curriculum which they will receive in later years' (HMI 1989a: para 65). We have explored elsewhere in the book the dangers of 'too formal, too soon' approaches to early education. Nor do we want 3–4-year-olds studying what are strangely defined as pre-reading, pre-maths or pre-science in a subject-specific way. The NCC document (NCC, 1989a), however, makes the important distinction between the inappropriateness of pre-fives being offered 'the curriculum – from the point of view of the learner – as separate subjects', and stresses at the same time that the *teacher* be aware of what strands underly the various collaborative, exploratory, manipulative and imaginative play situations in which the pupils engage. In this way a teacher can 'use the spontaneity and enthusiasm of young children to provide starting points for further work' while at the same time establishing a sense of continuity and progression with the framework prescribed by the National Curriculum.

The discussion of the beginnings of the National Curriculum have heightened awareness of the difficulty of defining 'good practice' in infant schools. But we probably know even less about what constitutes 'good practice' in the education of 3–5-year-olds. The different forms of educational provision offered to our pre-fives reflect the confused results of the uneven, unequal and unfair funding arrangements and resources provided by the local authorities across the country or dictated by the *laissez-faire* approach towards nursery education of central government policies. Moreover, different beliefs and practices emanating from past policies and ideologies in early years educational and childcare provision are reflected in the confusion amongst teachers of under-fives as to appropriate curriculum models they should be offering. In many reception classes 4-year-olds are being offered a pale reflection of the British nursery school tradition of structured play provision and practical or individual activities in baking, sand and water play, craftwork, table-top toys, etc.; a tradition which sits uncomfortably in infant classrooms, as we have indicated, alongside the elementary school tradition of teaching the basics of literacy and numeracy. The USA tradition of a 'cognitively orientated' curriculum such as High/Scope coexists uneasily with the Developmental Curriculum with its emphasis on children moving freely around self-chosen practical learning activities. Some nursery classes attached to primary schools have moved to a thematic approach to planning to fit in with the demands of their infant teacher colleagues. In the day care centres the staff place heavy emphasis on the physical and social well-being of the child, with perhaps the most structured teaching time being devoted to language development. Children are likely to meet any one or a combination of these curriculum models before they filter into the National Curriculum at 5. Or their parents may decide to exercise their right to keep the child at home until their fifth birthday.

But if we have legislated for an entitlement to a National Curriculum at 5, should there not also be an entitlement to a recognized quality of pre-fives' educational experiences formally defined by central government? We know that there is likely to be a rapid expansion of day care provision as the demand for labour in the 1990s encourages women with young children to return quickly to work. There is evidence that children most at risk to a 'poor start' to school (and consequently to the rigours of the National Curriculum) are those from disadvantaged homes (Mortimore and Blackstone 1982) and/or those who attend day nursery provision (Osborn and Milbank 1987). How then can we ensure that there is, as far as possible, equal access to the kind of pre-school education which will alleviate the chances of a 'poor start'?

In the first instance, there must be more research in the UK educational system into the long-term effects of different kinds of pre-school provision on the educational achievements of children. With hard data, rather than vague aspirations, at their disposal, the various vested interests dealing with under-fives – playgroup associations, social services, local education authorities, private day care providers – might be able to offer clear statements as to what constitutes effective pre-school education. A start has already been made in adopting a multidimensional approach by the National Children's Bureau. The Bureau has been publishing a range of influential materials for some time, but two recent publications from the Under Fives Unit are particularly helpful – *Early Childhood Education: The Early Years and the National Curriculum* (Early Years Curriculum Group 1989) and *Working with Children: Developing a Curriculum for the Early Years* (Drummond *et al.* 1989).

It is also important that initial teacher training courses acknowledge the training requirements of a multi-professional approach to working with under-fives. Teachers of young children must know how to supervise and train other workers in nursery and reception classes. They must also be taught the skills of professional liaison with social workers, health visitors, day care staff and local clinics. In many initial training courses for the teachers of under-fives, these issues are scarcely addressed.

The 1990s and beyond

The three issues of assessment, special educational needs and a curriculum for the under-fives are just three amongst the many concerns preoccupying infant teachers as they struggle to adapt to the new demands put upon them by the Education Reform Act. The levels of stress in infant schools are high. There simply is too much coming at the teachers too fast. Nevertheless, because of their commitment to the children, infant teachers are struggling to keep abreast of the changes demanded of them. There is a great resilience there – perhaps because the work-force is predominantly women and women are well versed in the arts of personal survival! But infant teachers are particularly alarmed by the politicizing of education. They feel threatened by the 'male' business world jargon – audit returns, consumers, performance indicators, loss leaders – which is increasingly and, they feel, inappropriately applied to the education of children. It is designed to intimidate.

I do not think that we should be afraid of the changes. We have already seen that classroom practice is immensely resistant to changes initiated from outside rather than inside the classroom. I like to remember the image of a group of Cherokee Indians who were baffled when some well-meaning American administrators were anxiously planning to protect from the ravages of the weather the totem pole they had newly carved for a Red Indian Cultural Centre. The Cherokees simply said that it did not matter if the totem pole weathered. First of all, that was the way totem poles were. Second, when the pole began to crumble away they would always know how to carve another one, a variation perhaps on their newly finished design.

The theme of the changes and continuities in infant schooling explored in this book could be represented by the metaphor of that totem pole, open to the effects of forces from outside, but at the heart belonging to the craft knowledge and quiet confidence of the generations of Indians who had gone before. In the end it is the teachers who form the heart of any educational system. What matters is that they are not afraid to address in an analytical way the kinds of dilemmas identified in this book, and to create new ways of working which maintain a respect for their own culture, traditions, and craft knowledge. I hope that infant teachers will be given the personal and professional space they deserve to do exactly that.

References

Alexander, R. (1984) *Primary Teaching*, Eastbourne: Holt, Rinehart & Winston.
Alexander, R., Wilcocks, J. and Kinder, K. (1989) *Changing Primary Practice*, Lewes: Falmer Press.
Anning, A. (1987) 'An analysis of primary teachers' understanding of how children learn and its relationship to their teaching strategies', unpublished MEd thesis, University of Leicester.
Anning, A. (1988) 'Teachers' theories about children's learning', in J. Calderhead (ed.) *Teachers' Professional Development*, Lewes: Falmer Press.
Anning, A. and Gates, J. (1989) 'The National Curriculum and good infant practice', *Education 3–13* 17, 3: 25–8.
Anning, A., Brown, D., Galton, M. and Kinch, T. (1986) 'Attitudes and the infant teacher: conflicts in society', *Child Education* June: 15–22.
Argyris, C. and Schon, D. A. (1976) *Theory in Practice: Increasing Professional Effectiveness*, San Francisco: Jossey-Bass.
Ashton, P., Kneen, P., Davies, F. and Holley, B. (1975) *The Aims of Primary Education: A Study of Teachers' Opinions*, London and Basingstoke; Macmillan Education for Schools Council.
APU (Assessment of Performance Unit) (1984) *Science in Schools Age 11: Report No 4*, London: HMSO.
Athey, C. (1980) 'Parental involvement in nursery education', *Early Childhood* 1, 3, December: 2–8.
Athey, C. (1981) 'Parental involvement in nursery education', in R. Evans (ed.) *Early Childhood Development and Care* 7, 4: 253–67.
Auld, R. (1976) *William Tyndale Junior and Infants Schools Public Inquiry*, London: ILEA.
Barrett, G. (1986) *Starting School; An Evaluation of the Experience*, School of Education, Unversity of East Anglia.
Barrie, J. M. (1915) *Peter Pan and Wendy; The Story of Peter Pan extracted from Peter*

and Wendy, illustrated by P. D. Bedford, authorized school edn. London: Henry Frowde/Hodder & Stoughton.

Barrow, R. (1984) *Giving Teaching Back to Teachers*, Brighton: Wheatsheaf.

Bassey, M. (1978) *Nine Hundred Primary School Teachers*, Windsor: NFER.

Bennett, D. (1987) 'The aims of teachers and parents for children in their first year at school', in *Four Year Olds in School: Policy and Practice*, NFER/SCDC Report, Windsor: NFER.

Bennett, J. (1979) *Learning to Read with Picture Books*, Gloucester: Thimble Press.

Bennett, N. (1976) *Teaching Styles and Pupil Progress*, London: Open Books.

Bennett, N. and Kell, J. (1989) *A Good Start: Four Year Olds in Infant Schools*, Oxford: Basil Blackwell.

Bennett, N., Desforges, C., Cockburn, A. and Wilkinson, B. (1984) *The Quality of Pupil Learning Experiences*, London: Lawrence Erlbaum

Bereiter, C. and Engelmann, S. (1966) *Teaching Disadvantaged Children in Pre-School*, Englewood Cliffs, NJ: Prentice-Hall.

Berlak, A. and Berlak, H. (1981) *Dilemmas of Schooling: Teaching and Social Change*, London: Methuen.

Bernstein, B. B. (1971, 1975) *Class, codes and controls*, Vol. 1 and 3, London: Routledge & Kegan Paul.

Blenkin, G. V. and Kelly, A. V. (eds) (1987) *Early Childhood Education: A Developmental Curriculum*, London: Paul Chapman.

Blyth, J. E. (1984) *Place and Time with Children Five to Nine*, Beckenham: Croom Helm.

Blyth, W. A. L. (1976) *Place Time and Society 8–13: Curriculum Planning in History, Geography and Social Science*, Glasgow and Bristol: Collins/ESL.

Blyth, W. A. L. (1984) *Development, Experience and Curriculum in Primary Education*, Beckenham: Croom Helm.

Board of Education (1931) *Report of the Consultative Committee on the Primary School*, Hadow Report, London: HMSO.

Board of Education (1933) *Report of the Consultative Committee on Infant and Nursery Schools*, London: HMSO.

Brearley, M., Bott, R., Davies, M. P., Glynne-Jones, M. L., Hitchfield, E. M., Johnson, J. E. L. and Tamburrini, J. R. (1969) *Fundamentals in the First School*, Oxford: Basil Blackwell.

Brittan, E. M. (1976) 'Multicultural education 2. Teacher opinion and aspects of school life. Part One: changes in curriculum and school organisation', *Educational Research* 18, 2: 96–116.

Brown, G. and Desforges, C. (1979) *Piaget's Theory: a Psychological Critique*, London: Routledge & Kegan Paul.

Browne, N. and France, P. (1986) 'Only cissies wear dresses: a look at sexist talk in the nursery', in G. Weiner (ed.) *Just a Bunch of Girls*, Milton Keynes: Open University Press.

Bruner, J. S. (1960) *The Process of Education*, Cambridge, Mass.: Harvard University Press.

Bruner, J. S. (1966) *Towards a Theory of Instruction*, Cambridge, Mass.: Harvard University Press.

Bruner, J. S. (1972) 'Functions of plays', in Bruner (ed.) *Play*, Harmondsworth: Penguin.

Bruner, J. S. (1980) *Under Five in Britain*, Oxford Pre-School Research Project, London: Grant McIntyre.

Bruner, J. S. and Haste, H. (eds) (1987) *Making Sense: The Child's Construction of the World*, London: Methuen.

Buxton, L. G. (1982) 'Emotional responses to symbolism', *Visible Language* XVI, 3: 215–20.

Campbell, R. J. (1985) *Developing the Primary School Curriculum*, London: Holt, Rinehart & Winston.

CACE (Central Advisory Council for Education, England) (1967) *Children and their Primary Schools*, Plowden Report, London: HMSO.

Chazan, M., Laing, A. and Harper, G. (1987) *Teaching Five to Eight Year Olds*, Oxford: Basil Blackwell.

Chomsky, N. (1976) *Reflections on Language*, London: Fontana.

Clarricoates, K. (1980) 'The importance of being Ernest, Emma, Tom, John . . .', in R. Deem (ed.) *Schooling for Women's Work*, London: Routledge & Kegan Paul.

Clay, M. (1975) *What Did I Write?*, London: Heinemann Educational.

Clay, M. (1979) *Reading: The Patterning of Complex Behaviour*, London: Heinemann Educational.

Cleave, S., Jowett, S. and Bate, M. (1982) *And So To School: A Study of Continuity from Pre-School to Infant School*, Windsor: NFER/Nelson.

Clift, P., Cleave, S. and Griffin, M. (1980) *The Aims, Role and Deployment of Staff in the Nursery*, Report of the National Foundation of Educational Research in England and Wales, Windsor: NFER.

Coe, J. (1966) 'The junior school: approaches to non-streaming' *Forum* 8: 76–9.

Copple, C., Sigal, I. E. and Saunders, R. (1979) *Educating the Young Thinker: Classroom Strategies for Cognitive Growth*, New York: D. Van Nostrand.

Corsaro, W. A. (1979) '"We're friendly, right?" Children's use of access rituals in a nursery school', *Language in Society* 8: 315–36.

Cowie, H. (ed.) (1984) *The Development of Children's Imaginative Writing*, London: Croom Helm.

Cox, G. B. and Dyson, A. C. (eds) (1971) *The Black Papers in Education*, London: Davis-Poynter.

Csiksentmihalyi, M. T. (1979) 'The concept of flow in play', in B. Sutton Smith (ed.) *Play and Learning*, New York: Gardner Press.

Curtis, S. J. and Boultwood, M. E. A. (1962) *An Introductory History of English Education since 1800*, 2nd edn, London: University Tutorial Press.

Dearden, R. F. (1968) *The Philosophy of Primary Education*, London, Routledge & Kegan Paul.

De Lyon, H. and Migniuolo, F. (eds) (1989) *Women Teachers*, Milton Keynes: Open University Press.

DES (1977a) *A New Partnership for Our Schools*, Taylor Report, London: HMSO.

DES (1977b) Circular 14/77, London: HMSO.

DES (1978a) *Primary Education in England: A Survey by HM Inspectors of Schools*, London: HMSO.

DES (1978b) *Special Educational Needs*, Warnock Report, London: HMSO.

DES (1979) *A Framework for the School Curriculum*, London: HMSO.

DES (1981a) *The School Curriculum*, London: HMSO.

DES (1981b) *West Indian Children in Our Schools*, Interim Report of the Committee of

Enquiry into the education of children from ethnic minority groups, the Rampton Report, London: HMSO.

DES (1982a) *Education 5 to 9: An Illustrative Survey of 80 First Schools in England*, London: HMSO.

DES (1982b) *Mathematics Counts*, Cockcroft Report, London: HMSO.

DES (1983) *Assessment and Statements of Special Educational Needs*, Circular 1/83, London: HMSO.

DES (1984) *Educational Support Grants*, Circular 6/84, London: HMSO.

DES (1985a) *Better Schools*, White Paper Cmnd 9469, London: HMSO.

DES (1985b) *The Curriculum from 5 to 16*, Curriculum Matters 2, HMI series, London: HMSO.

DES (1985c) *Science 5–16: A Statement of Policy*, London: HMSO.

DES (1987) *Educational Reform: Government Proposals for Schools*, London: HMSO.

DES (1988a) *National Curriculum Task Group on Assessment and Testing: A Report*, London: HMSO.

DES (1988b) *DES Statistical Bulletin 7/88, Pupils Under Five Years in Local Education Authority in England, January 1988*, London: HMSO.

DES (1989a) *National Curriculum: From Policy to Practice*, London: HMSO.

DES (1989b) *Aspects of Primary Education: The Teaching and Learning of Science*, London: HMSO.

DES (1989c) *The Teaching and Learning of History and Geography*, London: HMSO.

DES (1989d) Circular No 5/89, *Education Reform Act 1988, The School Curriculum and Assessment*, 22 Feb 1989, DES Publications.

DES (1989e) Statistical Bulletin 7/89, London: HMSO.

DES/WO (1987) *The National Curriculum 5–16: A Consultative Document*, London: HMSO.

Desforges, C. and Cockburn, A. (1987) *Understanding the Mathematics Teacher: A Study of Practice in First Schools*, Lewes: Falmer Press.

Donaldson, M. (1978) *Children's Minds*, Glasgow: Fontana/Collins.

Driver, R. (1983) *The Pupil as Scientist*, Milton Keynes: Open University Press.

Drummond, M. J., Lally, M. and Pugh, G. (eds) (1989) *Working with Children, Developing a curriculum for the Early Years*, Under Fives Unit, National Children's Bureau, Nottingham: Nottingham Group/NCB.

Early Years Curriculum Group (1989) *Early Childhood Education, The Early Years and the National Curriculum*, Stoke-on-Trent: Trentham Books Ltd.

Edwards, A. D. and Westgate, D. P. G. (1987) *Investigating Classroom Talk*, Lewes: Falmer Press.

Egan, K. (1988) 'The origins of the imagination and the curriculum', in K. Egan and D. Nadamer (eds) *Imagination and Education*, Milton Keynes: Open University Press.

Engelmann, S., Osborn, J. and Engelmann, T. (1972) *DISTAR Learning Program*, Chicago, Ill.: Science Research Associates.

Froebel, F. W. (1826) *The Education of Man*, New York: Appleton.

Gage, N. (1985) *Hard Gains in the Soft Sciences: The Case of Pedagogy*, CEOR Monograph, Bloomington, Ind.: Phi Delta Kappa.

Galton, M. (1987) 'An ORACLE chronicle: a decade of classroom research', *Teaching and Teacher Education* 3, 4: 299–314.

Galton, M. (1989) *Teaching in the Primary School*, London: David Fulton.

Galton, M. and Simon, B. (1980) *Progress and Performance in the Primary Classroom*, London: Routledge & Kegan Paul.

Galton, M., Simon, B. and Croll, P. (1980) *Inside the Primary Classroom*, London: Routledge & Kegan Paul.

Garvey, C. (1977) *Play*, London: Fontana/Open Books.

Gilligan, C. (1982) *In a Different Voice*, Cambridge, Mass.: Harvard University Press.

Golby, M. (1988) 'Traditions in primary education', in M. Clarkson (ed.) *Emerging Issues in Primary Education*, Lewes: Falmer Press.

Goldstein, W., Underwood, M., Bysouth, J. and Rabinowitz, A. I. (1984) *Classroom Observation Procedure*, ILEA: Schools Psychological Service.

Good, T. and Brophy, J. (1986) 'Teacher behaviour and student achievement', in M. Wittrock (ed.) *Handbook of Research on Teaching*, 3rd edn, New York: Macmillan.

Hall, N. (1987) *The Emergence of Literacy*, UKRA Teaching of Reading Monography, London: Edward Arnold.

Harlen, W., Darwin, A. and Murphy, M. (1977a) *Asking Questions: A Leader's Guide*, Edinburgh: Oliver & Boyd.

Harlen, W., Darwin, A. and Murphy, M. (1977b) *Finding Answers: Match and Mismatch*, Edinburgh: Oliver & Boyd.

Haste, H. (1987) 'Growing into rules', in J. S. Bruner and H. Haste (eds) *Making Sense: The Child's Construction of the World*, London: Methuen.

Hegarty, S., Pocklington, K. and Lucas, D. (1981) *Educating Pupils with Special Needs in the Ordinary School*, Windsor: NFER/Nelson.

Hirst, P. H. (1974) *Knowledge and the Curriculum*, London: Routledge & Kegan Paul.

HMI (1989a) *The Education of Children Under Five*, London: HMSO.

HMI (1989b) *Report by HM Inspectors on a Survey of the Quality of Education for Four Year Olds in Primary Classes – Reference 339/89/NS*, London: DES.

Hohmann, M., Banet, B. and Weikart, D. P. (1979) *Young Children in Action*, Ypsilanti, Mich.: High/Scope Press.

Holt, J. (1968) *How Children Learn*, London: Pitman.

Holt, J. (1984) *How Children Fail*, revised edn, Harmondsworth: Penguin.

Hughes, M. (1986) *Children and Number*, Oxford: Basil Blackwell.

ILEA (1978) *People Around Us: Unit 1: Families*; (1979) *People Around Us: Unit 2: Friends*; (1980) *People Around Us: Unit 3: Work*; London: ILEA and A. & C. Black.

ILEA (1987) *The Early Years: A Curriculum for Young Children*, London: ILEA Centre for Learning Resources.

Isaacs, S. (1929) *The Nursery Years*, London: Routledge & Kegan Paul.

Isaacs, S. (1948) *Childhood and After*, London: Routledge & Kegan Paul.

Kerr, J. F. (ed.) (1968) *Changing the Curriculum*, London: University of London Press.

King, R. (1978) *All Things Bright and Beautiful? A Sociological Study of Infants' Classrooms*, Bath: John Wiley.

Klein, M. (1949) *The Psycho Analysis of Children*, trans. A. Stracey, 3rd edn, London: International Psycho-analytical Library 22.

Kohlberg, L. (1976) 'Moral stages and moralization: the cognitive-developmental approach', in T. Lickona (ed.) *Moral Development and Behaviour*, New York: Holt, Rinehart & Winston.

Lawton, D. (1980) *The Politics of the School Curriculum*, London: Routledge & Kegan Paul.

Little, A. and Willey, R. (1983) *Studies in the Multi-Ethnic Curriculum*, London: Schools Council.

Lowenfeld, M. (1935) *Play in Childhood*, London: Gollancz.

McCutcheon, G. (1980) 'How do elementary teachers plan? The nature of planning and the influences on it', *Elementary School Journal* 81, 1: 5–9.

Mackay, D., Thompson, B. and Schaub, P. (1970) *Breakthrough to Literacy*, Teachers' Manual, Harlow: Longman.

McMillan, M. (1923) *Education Through Imagination*, London: Deit.

Manzer, R. A. (1970) *Teachers and Politics*, Manchester: Manchester University Press.

Marshall, S. (1963) *An Experiment in Education*, Cambridge: Cambridge University Press.

Meadows, S. and Cashdan, A. (1983) *Teaching Styles in Nursery Education*, London final report to SSRC, unpublished.

Meadows, S. and Cashdan, A. (1988) *Helping Children Learn, Contributions to a Cognitive Curriculum*, London: David Fulton.

Millar, S. (1968) *The Psychology of Play*, Harmondsworth: Penguin.

Montessori, M. (1972) *Dr. Montessori's Own Handbook*, first published in English 1914, New York: Schocken Books.

Mortimore, P. and Blackstone, T. (1982) *Education and Disadvantage*, London: Heinemann.

Mullin, B., Morgan, V. and Dunn, S. (1986) *Gender Differentiation in Infant Classes*, University of Ulster at Coleraine, Northern Ireland: Equal Opportunities Commission.

Nash, R. C. (1973) *Classrooms Observed*, London: Routledge & Kegan Paul.

NCC (National Curriculum Council) (1989a) *A Framework for the Primary Curriculum*, York: NCC.

NCC (1989b) *National Curriculum: From Policy to Practice*, National Curriculum Information Pack 1, York: NCC.

NCC (1989c) Circular 5/89 *Education Reform Act: The School Curriculum and Assessment*, 22 Feb 1989, York: NCC.

NCC (1989e) Circular no 5. *Implementing the National Curriculum: Participation by Pupils with Special Educational Needs*, May 1989, York: NCC.

NCC/WO (National Curriculum Council/Welsh Office) (1989a) *English in the National Curriculum*, London: HMSO.

NCC/WO (1989b) *Mathematics in the National Curriculum*, London: HMSO.

NCC/WO (1989c) *Science in the National Curriculum*, London: HMSO.

NCC/WO (1989d) *Design and Technology for ages 5–16*, York: NCC.

NCC/WO (1989e) *Technology 5–16 in the National Curriculum*, November 1989 York: NCC.

NEU (National Education Union) (1870) *A Verbatim Report of the Debate in Parliament during the Progress of the Elementary School Bill*, reported in N. Whitbread (1972) *The Evolution of the Nursery Infant School*, London: Routledge & Kegan Paul.

NFER/SCDC (National Foundation for Educational Research/Schools Curriculum Development Council) (1987) *Four Year Olds in School: Policy and Practice*, Windsor: NFER.

Nelson, K. (1977) 'Cognitive development and the acquisition of concepts', in R. C. Anderson, R. J. Spiro and W. E. Montegue (eds) *Schooling and the Acquisition of Knowledge*, Hillsdale NJ: Lawrence Erlbaum.

Newcastle Commission (1861) *Royal Commission Report*, Newcastle Commission (Elementary Education).

Newson, E. and Newson, J. (1977) *Perspectives on School at Seven Years Old*, London: Allen & Unwin

Nias, J. (1988) 'Informal primary education in action: teacher accounts', in W. A. L. Blyth (ed.) *Informal Primary Education Today*, Lewes: Falmer Press.

Nias, J. (1989) *Teachers Talking: A Study of Teaching as Work*, London: Routledge & Kegan Paul.

Nicholls, R. (1986) (ed.) *Rumpus Schema Extra*, January, Saltburn Cleveland LEA.

Osborn, A. F. and Milbank, J. E. (1987) *The Effects of Early Education*, Report from the Child Health and Education Study, Oxford: Clarendon Press.

Peters, R. S. (1966) *Ethics and Education*, London: Allen & Unwin.

Piaget, J. (1932) *The Moral Judgement of the Child*, London: Routledge & Kegan Paul.

Piaget, J. (1962) *Play, Dreams and Imitation in Childhood*, New York: Norton.

Piaget, J. (1971) *Science of Education and the Psychology of the Child*, London: Longman.

Piaget, J. (1977) *The Moral Judgement of the Child*, Harmondsworth; Penguin.

Piaget, J. and Inhelder, B. (1956) *The Child's Conception of Space*, London: Routledge & Kegan Paul.

Pilling, D. and Kellmer Pringle, M. (1978) *Controversial Issues in Child Development*, London: Paul Elek for National Children's Bureau.

Pollard, A. (1985) *The Social World of the Primary School*, Eastbourne: Holt, Rinehart & Winston.

Pollard, A. (1987) 'Coping strategies and the multiplication of differentiation in infant classes', in A. Cohen and L. Cohen (eds) *Early Education: The School Years*, London: Paul Chapman.

Prindep (1989) *Changing Classroom Practice: Decisions and Dilemmas*, Prindep, 110 Merrion House, Leeds, LS2 8DT.

Reid, J. and Donaldson, M. (1979) *The Written Word: Teachers' Manual to Link Up Reading Scheme*, Edinburgh: Holmes McDougall.

Richards, C. (1982) *Primary Education 1974–80*, in Richards, C. (ed.) *New Directions in Primary Education*, Lewes: Falmer Press.

Robinson, K. (ed.) (1982) *The Arts in School*, Gulbenkian Report, London: Calouste Gulbenkian Foundation.

Rosen, H. (1984) *The Nurture of Narratives: Stories and Meanings*, London: National Association for the Teaching of English.

Rosenshine, B. (1987) 'Direct instruction', in M. Dunkin (ed.) *Teaching and Teacher Education*, Oxford: Pergamon Press.

Rousseau, J. J. (1762) *Emile, Book 2*, quoted in P. Abbs (ed.) (1987) *The Living Powers*, Lewes: Falmer Press.

Rubin, Z. (1980) *Children's Friendships*, London: Fontana.

Rudduck, J. (1986) 'Curriculum change: management and meaning?', *School Organization* 6, 1: 107–15.

SEAC (Schools Examination and Assessment Council) (July 1989a) Letter and Circular NCA/7/19–24 from Philip Halsey to Kenneth Baker, London: SEAC.

SEAC (1989b) *A Guide to Teacher Assessment*, Packs A, B and C, London: Heinemann for SEAC.

Sharp, R. and Green, A. (1975) *Education and Social Control: A Study in Progressive Primary Education*, London: Routledge & Kegan Paul.

Sinclair, J. McH. and Coulthard, R. M. (1975) *Towards an Analysis of Discourse: The English Used by Teachers and Pupils*, London: Oxford University Press.

Skinner, B. F. (1974) *About Behaviourism*, London: Cape.

Smith, F. (1971) *Understanding Reading*, New York: Holt, Rinehart & Winston.

Smith, F. (1978) *Reading*, Cambridge: Cambridge University Press.

Smith, F. (1982) *Writing and the Writer*, London: Heinemann Educational.

Smith, P. K. and Cowie, H. (1988) *Understanding Children's Development*, Oxford: Basil Blackwell.

Southgate, V., Arnold, H., and Johnson, S. (1981) *Extending Beginning Reading*, London: Heinemann for the Schools Council.

Spencer, C., Blade, M. and Morsley, K. (1990) *The Child and the Physical Environment*, Chichester: John Wiley.

Spender, D. (1982) *Invisible Women: The Schooling Scandal*, London: Writers & Readers.

Spock, B. (1946) *Baby and Child Care*, New York: Pocket Books.

Stannard, J. (1988) 'Focus on the Curriculum 3–7', *Child Education* September: 8–9.

Steiner, R. (1926) *The Essentials of Education*, London: Anthroposophical Publishing.

Stones, E. (1984) *Supervision in Teacher Education*, London: Methuen.

Swann Committee (1985) *Education for All*, Swann Report, Cmnd 9453, London: HMSO.

Sylva, K., Roy, C. and Painter, M. (1980) *Childwatching at Playgroup and Nursery School*, London: Grant McIntyre.

Tann, C. S. (1981) 'Grouping and group work', in B. Simon and J. Willcocks (eds) *Research and Practice in the Primary Classroom*, London: Routledge & Kegan Paul.

Taylor, P. H., Exon, G. and Holley, B. (1972) *A Study of Nursery Education*, Schools Council Working Paper 41, London: Evans/Methuen Educational.

Times Educational Supplement (1990) *Tests Fail to Jolt Real-Book Faithful*, 27 July 1990: 4.

Tizard, B. and Hughes, M. (1984) *Young Children Learning: Talking and Listening at Home and at School*, London: Fontana.

Tizard, J., Schofield, W. N. and Hewison J. (1982) 'Collaboration between teachers and parents in assisting children's reading', *British Journal of Educational Psychology* 52: 1–15.

Tizard, B., Blatchford, P., Burke, J., Farquar, C. and Plewis, I. (1988) *Young Children at School in the Inner City*, Hove: Lawrence Erlbaum.

Topping, K. (1984) 'Paired reading', *Child Education*, December: 10–11.

Topping, K. (1985) 'Paired reading', *Child Education*, January: 10–11.

Tough, J. (1976) *Listening to Children Talking*, London: Ward Lock Educational.

Turiel, E. (1978) 'Distinct conceptual and development Domains: social convention and morality', in S. Meadows (1986) Understanding Child Development, London: Hutchinson Education, p. 235.

Tyler, R. W. (1949) *Basic Principles of Curriculum and Instruction*, Chicago, Ill.: University of Chicago Press.

Van der Eycken, W. and Turner, B. (1969) *Adventures in Education*, London: Allen Lane.

Vygotsky, L. (1978) *Mind in Society* (edited by M. Cambridge, Mass.: Cole) Harvard University Press.

Walkerdine, V. (1985) *Psychological Knowledge and Educational Practice: Producing the Truth about Schools*, Bedford Way Papers 25, University of London, Institute of Education.

Waterland, L. C. (1985) *Read with Me: An Apprenticeship Approach to Reading*, Gloucester: Thimble Press.

Webb, L. (1974) *Purpose and Practice in Nursery Education*, Oxford: Basil Blackwell.

Weiner, G. (1985) *Just a Bunch of Girls*, Milton Keynes: Open University Press.

Wells, G. (1987) *The Meaning Makers*, Portsmouth: Hodder & Stoughton.

Whitbread, N. (1972) *The Evolution of the Nursery Infant School: A History of Infant and Nursery Education in Britain 1800–1970*, London: Routledge & Kegan Paul.

Whyte, J. (1983) *Beyond the Wendy House: Sex Role Stereotyping in Primary Schools*, York: Longman for Schools Council.

Wilkinson, A. (1986) *The Quality of Writing*, Milton Keynes: Open University Press.

Willes, M. J. (1983) *Children into Pupils*, London: Routledge & Kegan Paul.

Wolfendale, S. (1987) *All About Me*, produced in association with the Under Fives Unit, London: National Children's Bureau.

Young, M. F. D. (ed.) (1971) *Knowledge and Control*, London: Collier Macmillan.

Name index

Subject index